Making Waves

ANNA SEATON HUNTINGTON

Making Waves

The Inside Story of Managing and Motivating the First Women's Team to Compete for the America's Cup

THE SUMMIT PUBLISHING GROUP

THE SUMMIT PUBLISHING GROUP
One Arlington Centre
1112 East Copeland Road, Fifth Floor
Arlington, Texas 76011

Printed in the United States of America.

00 99 98 97 96   010   5 4 3 2 1

Library of Congress Cataloging-in-Publication Data

ISBN 1-56530-191-9
Cover and book design by David Sims
Photography by Daniel Forster

In Loving Memory of

Kirsten Pedersen,

"Powerful Katinka,"

My Mother

Table of Contents

Observations

by William I. Koch

The 1995 America's Cup women's team was by most measures a fabulous success. The very first race demonstrated that women are physically and mentally strong enough to compete head-to-head with men. The team expanded worldwide public interest in women's sports in general and sailing in particular. The media brought the women's team to millions of people around the world. It was even a commercial success. America³ Foundation raised more than $15 million and brought in totally new corporate sponsors to the America's Cup. America³ women's team members are regular crew on former all-male racing boats. Three members competed in the 1996 Olympics, two in sailing (one winning a bronze medal) and one in rowing. Even one crew member, Dawn Riley, has become the first woman to become an official challenger for the America's Cup. Overall, the team had a profound effect on women in sports.

The women, however, did not win the Cup, but even that turned out well. Dennis Conner, by beating the women in the finals, went on to the Cup final and endured "The Slaughter on the Water" from the Kiwis. If the women had won the last race and then been swept by the Kiwis, as Dennis was, the old guard at the yacht clubs would have had a field day saying, "If only Dennis's crew had been on the boat, America would have kept the Cup."

All the glorious things aside, what to me was the most worthwhile as well as most painful lesson was what we learned about managing men and women from the mistakes we made.

The women's team was not conceived as a feminist statement. Rather, it evolved from the America[3] philosophy that with the right focus, commitment, and teamwork, ordinary people can do extraordinary things. In 1992, Dawn Riley, as a member of the sailing crew, did her job better than any of the men, demonstrating that women could do it. In 1992, a women's team was attempted—the Pegasus Group—but it could not get off the ground because of a lack of support. The America's Cup is a race of management, money, technology, teamwork, and last and incidentally, sailing. After a market study showed that most Americans view the America's Cup as an elitist sport sailed in the backwaters of a snotty yacht club, it became clear that a women's team could greatly enhance the sport. It would create controversy in the sailing community since it was generally believed that women are not strong enough to handle a boat as well as men, and since it has always been considered bad luck to have women on board from the beginning of sailing. It would appeal to a broad audience since more than half of the world's population is women. And most important, by doing well the team would give credence to America[3]'s philosophy.

The idea was simple. Select a group of outstanding female athletes. Give them fast boats, a proven management team and organization with its extensive infrastructure, the best technology in the world, and train them the way the winning male team had been trained in 1992. Then, presto, we could have a winning women's team, the first in history, that could rock the world.

It did not work out that way. We, the male management, underestimated the cultural hurdles and biases that had to be overcome, and we made too many mistakes in handling sensitive and subtle male-female leadership differences. Generally, the team that wins is not the one that is most brilliant but the one that makes the fewest mistakes. Unfortunately, we did not realize the mistakes we were making until it was too late to do anything about it. It will be worth it if others can learn from our experiences.

As we were putting the team together, we contacted a number of experts on women and leadership. We also read all the books we could find on the subject. We brought in a number of accomplished women to explain to the crew what it takes to be successful in the real world. Based upon what these people said, and what we learned as we went along, we tried to modify the program that had worked so well with the men in 1992.

We observed some fascinating similarities and differences between the men's team and the women's team. The women took to coaching exceptionally well, and were eager to learn and improve, while the men almost refused to be coached: "If the coaches know so much, why aren't they out there winning the Cup?" The women did the routine chores of cleaning the boat, drying and packing the sails, repairing equipment, and getting the boat ready for the next day twice as fast as the men. Everyone helped. No job was beneath any of the women, and they organized themselves into efficient, small units. Many of the men had complained that those chores were too menial, that they had other, more important things to do, or spent hours debating whose technique was best to get the job done. The women were much more enthusiastic and more rigorous in their workout program than the men. They achieved an outstanding level of fitness and strength. A number of the women could bench press the weight of their husbands or significant others. Several could even clean-and-jerk the weight of their husbands.

On the race course, the women could mix it up with the best in the world and engage in a tacking duel until the other boat would call it off. They were mentally tough enough to ignore during the prestart maneuvers of each race the intimidation tactics of Paul Cayard and his crew, who were flipping them the bird and yelling obscenities. Most profoundly, the women as a group became a working team in less than a month after starting training; it had taken the men more than eighteen months, and it was well into the finals before we coalesced into a team.

The women wanted badly just to be sailors and competitors. When offered a portable potty, the women refused: "We will go over the side, only give us shirts with longer tails in case some spectators are close by." During the 6:30 A.M. workouts, some of the younger, single women would show up wearing T-shirts of some of the foreign teams. They could hold their own at a bar with the best of them. They became some of the best sailors and competitors in the world.

There were some differences to which the male coaches had trouble adjusting. Before the start of the 6:30 A.M. workouts there

was a warm-up period of ten minutes of light jogging or riding stationary bicycles. In 1992, the men would work through this period
very slowly and groggily, not saying a word. The women, who got
on the five stationary bicycles, would pedal vigorously and would
have at least ten animated conversations going on simultaneous-
ly. If, during a workout, a trainer yelled at a woman, scolding her
for not doing a correct push-up, she might run out of the gym cry-
ing. If, on the other hand, he got down on the floor and showed
how to do a push-up correctly, she would thank him and forever
more do correct push-ups. Once a woman came to the trainer,
complaining that she was slipping on the locker-room floors and
asked why he didn't put down rubber mats. He looked at her with
wide eyes and said, "Why don't you wear rubber thongs the way
men do." She replied, "OK. Good idea. Thanks."

The women bonded together and formed very strong friendships within cliques. They were reluctant to compete head-on with
one another for the spots on the boat. They also campaigned vigorously for their friends to be on the boat. One woman, who was
one of the best at her job, quit the team when her partner and
good friend in the pit was replaced by a more experienced and
accomplished woman. The men weren't that way. They had less
concern for who their teammates were as long as they themselves
were on the boat. When the women went to the coaches with a
problem, they appeared to be more interested in talking about
their problems than in coming to a solution. There was a constant
complaint that "the coaches did not respect our feelings."

The most baffling thing of all to the male leadership of
America[3] was the team's apparent reluctance to promote and
accept leadership from one of their own. Whereas men had tried

bullying their way into leadership positions, the women were equals and wanted to manage by consensus. The male management viewed the problems that led to a man being put on the team as simply a lack of leadership. First, give leadership authority to JJ as the tactician, and if she cannot handle it, then promote Leslie as skipper with authority over the tactician. If that does not work, put someone else on the boat who has leadership skills and does not clutch in tight situations. The coaches did not train anyone as a backup tactician, so our only alternative was to put one of the guest coaches on board. The women, on the other hand, viewed the problem that led to the changes as a personality conflict between JJ and Leslie.

The big mistakes that we made resulted from our male culture, especially our lack of understanding of the differences between men and women. The first mistake was our macho belief that our technology could produce a boat significantly faster than the competitors' without even tuning it properly instead of one that was equally fast or only marginally faster. Because of that, we delayed starting the program to gain a strong negotiating position with the San Diego Yacht Club and delayed until the last minute the delivery of the final boat to get more out of our tank and computer testing. Equally as important was on-the-water training time and optimization of the boats. Those boats are so sensitive, it takes a long time for even the most experienced sailor to learn how to sail them to their optimum, much less someone who has never been on a big boat before. In fact, the Kiwis spent one year sailing their final boats.

Mistakes were made in communicating with the team. The women focused on the emotions behind a communication rather than what was said. As with any group of people, when there was a conflict between what was said and what was practiced, they went with what was practiced. For example, when the team was told the designers wanted their input into the design of the boat, they said "great." But when no designer asked them specifically, they did not bother to volunteer any suggestions.

Furthermore, the fact that a clearly defined objective was not communicated to the organization caused a great deal of confusion. Were they all a women's team no matter what? Were they to win at all costs or somewhere in between?

Perhaps our biggest failure was the belief that a women's team could be managed by males using a system designed by males for males and could work even with absentee management. Both the chairman and the president of America[3] did not move out to San Diego until just weeks before the trials started. We had no women in the senior management structure, although about 40 percent of the organization was female. Even with all the outside experts, our perception of what had to be done was entirely male.

We initially thought that an all-female team's weaknesses would be physical strength, experience sailing at an America's Cup level, and ability to work as a team. To overcome this, we would put in a more strenuous strength program than the one in 1992 for the men, would have long and rigorous practice sessions from the very beginning on actual America's Cup boats, lots of sailing instructions, and constant reinforcement of the concepts of teamwork. We would also have sport psychologists and women experts to help out. We had planned not to select a first team until close to the finals, rotating the crew each series. This was a radical concept we had introduced in 1992, which had received much criticism but had produced two outstanding teams as a result of intense internal competition for crew positions and forced adaptation of the crew to changing conditions. The radical concept we had for 1995 was the introduction of coaches who would select the team, along the style of the NFL or NBA. It has long been the tradition in sailing that the skipper selects the crew. The simple idea was that from all this training and the natural internal competition, the best team with a natural leader would rise to the occasion, as it had for the males in 1992.

We selected coaches who had been teammates in 1992, and knew the rigors of the America's Cup. They were outstanding sailors and excellent instructors, but they had grown up in the traditions of the sport and had traditional male views of sailing competition. The sport of sailing does not have coaches, in the sense of NBA basketball or NFL football. As such, they were not trained in skills of putting together the right mix of talent and teamwork and using competition and motivation to get the best out of each individual.

When the coaches thought they observed the women becoming upset when yelled at, a common tradition in male athletics, they concluded the women needed to be pampered or would burst into tears. They also concluded that the women weren't tough enough to withstand the rigors of outright confrontation and competition internally for the positions on the boat. Therefore, the coaches, according to the traditions of the sport, picked a first team far too early and left petty politics as the only avenue for other crew members to compete for positions. For key spots, there were no trained backups. Even outstanding guest coaches were excluded from coaching the first team with the following reason: "They will upset the morale of the team, and it'll take days to get them back."

This excuse of "not upsetting the girls" led to a lot of bad decisions, including not replacing near the finals several women who were under-performing with highly motivated women from the reserve team. The coaches concentrated on strength training and sailing instruction. As a result, the women were not trained to deal with internal competition, conflict resolution, and leadership development.

On the race course, decisions have to be made instantly. There is no time for consensus-building. The crew has to respond to dramatic and sudden changes. The crew members must confront one another forcibly and yet work as a team and then be friends after the race is over. Intense competition is necessary for superior perfomance.

We desperately needed mature female leadership, not only on the sailing team but also on the coaching staff and in the upper management of the organization. Had we had such leadership, we could have recognized our problems and concentrated on fixing them.

From this experience, we have found that women can perform in traditional male tasks equally if not superior to men, but you cannot put women into a male system and expect them to do well. If you want good results, you have to change the system to accommodate women with their different methods of communication. You have to train women to respond to the harsh realities of competition and to confront one another without becoming enemies. Correspondingly, you need to train men to communicate better and work together.

Men and women need each other. Their strengths and weaknesses complement each other. Men should be more respectful of each other's feelings, and women need to make decisions without fear of hurting their friends' feelings. Men need to work better as teams, and women need to exert leadership. When you put women and men together, the problems arise from their different priorities, perceptions, and different methods of communication. However, if you can recognize and respect those differences, an organization of men and women working harmoniously together can easily beat one that is made up of exclusively men or women.

Editors Note: Mr. Koch was the winning America's Cup skipper in 1992. In 1995 he was chairman of the America³ Foundation. He is president of Oxbow Corporation and is chairman of the Kansas Crime Commission.

Acknowledgments

I thank Bill Koch for giving me the opportunity to write this book. I'm grateful for Nickie Flynn's editorial insight, guidance, and challenge, all reflected here. I thank my father, friends, and teammates who provided support and suggestions along the way. My grandfather's advice to "put my nose to any handy grindstone" was the best ever. Sam Freedman taught me "book writing" a long time ago, but he's still always reading over my shoulder. I thank Mark Murphy for his editing expertise and his kindness. Most of all, I am grateful to my husband, Stewart, who often would come home from a hard day at his own job as an editor to advise, edit, console, and cajole me. He has always made me laugh, think, and feel loved.

Introduction

The winds off San Diego were unusually high. Everything seemed to happen in fast forward, especially for me, a late arrival to America³, the women's team. Racing for the America's Cup, modern sport's oldest trophy—and the Super Bowl, the Everest of sailboat racing—would begin in a few weeks. I was in my third week of sailing, ever. An Olympic rower, I'd been recruited for my physical strength and competitive spirit, not my knowledge of the sea.

I struggled to keep my balance on the bobbing, slippery bow. Waves crashed over the sides; there was nothing to hold onto. Our boat, also called *America³*, was an elegant but fierce war machine—seventy-five feet of sleek, raw, inhospitable carbon fiber. We were carving a graceful but aggressive hairpin turn around a small orange buoy.

Ten stories up at the top of the mast, the head of the enormous, parachute-like spinnaker began its lofty free fall. The newly hoisted jib flapped loudly behind me. My heart started racing. Along with two of my teammates, I reached out over the side of the boat, grabbed hold of the bottom edge of the thin, nylon sail, and with both hands, yanked it toward me against the pressure of the wind.

We had to get the spinnaker down quickly because, despite the speed and gigantic dimensions of the boats, the America's Cup can be a game of inches. Our body weight on the bow, as well as the drag of the spinnaker, were incrementally slowing the boat.

Like a boxer throwing punches, I frantically grabbed fistfuls of the dropping sail and thrust them back to my teammate standing below deck inside the hatch.

Breathing hard, focused on gathering the spinnaker, I missed the call from the cockpit—"TACKING!" The jib came at me like a tornado on its way to the other side of the boat. I ducked. The line attached to the jib became taut as it swept behind the filling sail. It hit my shins with what felt like the force of a moving car, and, as I flew across the bow into the Pacific, I reached down and grabbed onto the line. When I came up for air, I was amazed to see the line still in my hands, pulling me along with the boat.

I hung on while someone hauled in the line, grabbed my hand, and suddenly I was back on board. My fleece and nylon foul-weather gear were soaked, my boots full of water. I was uninjured but embarrassed.

We were still sailing, though, and the practice continued, nearly uninterrupted. A few of the women who had been sailors forever took a moment to smile at me and tell me I'd done a good job. "Way to stay with the boat," they said.

Eventually, I smiled, too. The power of the boat and the force of the elements had gotten the best of me. In an odd way, I loved it.

Until then, sailing had seemed an endless list of technical terms and maneuvers. For the first time, I glimpsed the sport's unique demands for acute feel and anticipation. We were like sixteen jockeys on the back of a huge, spirited beast, which itself was moving at the whim of Mother Nature. It was obvious that delays and other mistakes could cost us more than victory.

That day in December 1994 was my baptism into the art and brutal fun of sailing, and the four months of racing that followed marked women's initiation into racing for the America's Cup, sailing's Holy Grail.

Thankfully, stories of women breaking through gender barriers are becoming more and more rare. But until our team entered the race nearly 150 years after it began, women hadn't managed to gain a toehold in the chase for the America's Cup. Women have been sailing competitively against men just as long as they have been breaking into other sports. And racing sailboats is more like racing Indy cars and thoroughbreds than like football or boxing. Wits and courage matter more than physical strength.

But America's Cup racing, internationally regarded as the pinnacle of the sport, has been cloistered inside the elite, clubby, wholly male-dominated world of yacht clubs. To this day, old-fashioned aristocratic order prevails in most of those clubs, and women's official roles are often limited to fashion shows and "girls' nights out." For a century and a half, women have merely stood by watching as men jousted for the Cup and have applauded sweetly as they ascended the victory platform.

When the women's team began training in June 1994, we launched into precarious waters. Only one of us had any America's Cup experience. Our all-male competition had years of Cup racing under their belts. Simply because it had never been done before, many people, including some within our own camp, initially had doubts that we could even manage to get the boat around the course, much less compete respectably against the men.

But in less than a year, our team learned mountains of lessons about the specialized America's Cup boats and maneuvers. Once we mastered the basics, we became intent on victory. We silenced the naysayers in our first race when we barged onto the course and defeated Dennis Conner, one of the biggest names in sailing.

As the arduous and often controversial months of racing unfolded, we made mistakes, but we tenaciously hung on. Our task was complicated by the fact that the very apple cart we were intent on upsetting also happened to be our feeding trough. The women's team was a revolutionary concept in the America's Cup context, but behind the scenes we were owned, managed, and coached by men. In the end, we didn't win, but we'd done something no one had ever done before, and we were smiling, eager for more.

A Matter of Respect

The hand of Mr. America's Cup himself was limp in mine after I had offered a handshake in concession of defeat. Dennis Conner, shoulders and eyes averted, took only my fingers and shook lightly from the wrist. During racing, when our boats had whooshed past each other, inches apart, I had sneaked glances at this man. His well-tanned, once handsome, now bloated features were always calm. I could never read him. Was I seeing competitive confidence or a benign disguise for his real fear of losing to a boat sailed by women?

Now, as Dennis ever so gingerly shook my hand—as if I was a woman but not a real sailor—I had a sinking feeling that his expression was simply a sign of arrogance and that my team's year of struggle for respect as well as victory had been for naught.

The women of the America³ organization, Dennis's team, and the other U.S. America's Cup contender, PACT '95, were gathered at San Diego Yacht Club to crown Dennis the winner of our competition and defender of the Cup. After four months and nearly sixty races among the three teams in early 1995, Team Dennis Conner had managed, just the day before, to squeeze past America³'s *Mighty Mary* to win the final, deciding race. Officially dubbed the best in the country, Dennis would go on to unsuccessfully battle Team New Zealand, the best of seven foreign challengers, for the Cup.

After the speeches were given and the medals were awarded, fifty-two-year-old Dennis held court in the bar with his young wife, Daintry, while oysters, champagne, and dinner were served in the large dining room. I had joined others from the crowd who casually approached him to offer congratulations.

The Man to Beat

For the twenty-eight members of the women's team—a group of Cup rookies who, through sheer will and abundant faith, had transformed themselves into a viable contender, conceding defeat to big, bad "D.C." was quite unpleasant. For me, a newcomer to sailing, losing to Dennis Conner was one of those painfully regrettable times when Goliath had won. Dennis was a four-time America's Cup champion. The man to beat. The man to hate. He'd been uncivil toward our team on more than one occasion. Before the racing even began, he had snubbed our helmsperson, Leslie Egnot, backstage before a joint television appearance. At the start of several races, his crew had yelled obscenities and made indecent gestures at our team. All this—combined with Dennis's roly-poly appearance and high, squeaky voice—made "the Fat Man" an obnoxious but convenient rival. Beating him became a justifiable obsession for most of us.

For the majority of women on the team, those who had grown up racing sailboats, the awards ceremony was an emotionally wrenching occasion. Most had never dared dream of entering the previously all-male bastion of America's Cup racing. Therefore, they had a lifetime of appreciation for what it meant to come so close to defeating the man who had dominated the sport for decades, and whose name had become synonymous with the America's Cup.

After having engaged in more than twenty highly competitive races with us, I naively thought, Dennis might show the women's crew some new-found respect. We were, after all, not the only team eliminated in the preliminary racing. Seven teams of men, from the United States and around the world, had also fallen short in their quests for the America's Cup. But only the *Mighty Mary* crew risked being dismissed as a high-profile novelty—and a mistake—by los-

DENNIS CONNER

ing. *The men lost because their boats weren't fast; the women lost because they were, well, women.*

And it wasn't just Dennis. Sexist jokes flew around the yacht club that evening. Mocking photos of male sailors wearing dresses and displaying enormous breasts were not-so-surreptitiously passed around. As I walked toward Dennis in the darkened bar, I saw gloating relief spread across the tanned faces of table after table of silver-haired, blue-blazered men. Finally, that ridiculous women's team was out of their hair, they seemed to say. I imagined similar scenes in yacht clubs throughout the country: The old-timers smugly sipping celebratory cocktails, content that their world—where men take the helm and women organize the charity balls—was back in order.

I watched Dennis shake hands with David Dellenbaugh, the tactician and the only man on *Mighty Mary*. The gesture was natural and fluid between the two men. They looked each other in the eye and, as they shook hands, said without words—"until we meet again."

But I witnessed no such wholehearted connection between Dennis and any of the women from our team. When I shook his hand, his eyes met mine only briefly and then continued to scan the room. Despite heated races between us, he displayed no respect for us as equals. I tried to be a good sport and concede graciously, but I also felt the battle wasn't over. As far as I could tell, Dennis wouldn't even acknowledge that the battle had ever existed.

A Cup for the Wealthy Elite

The America's Cup—an elaborate Victorian silver pitcher standing more than two feet high and weighing just less than nine pounds—is modern sport's oldest trophy. The tradition of racing every three or four years for the Cup began nearly a century and a half ago. In 1851, *America*, a schooner representing the best of its young country's boat design and building capabilities, defeated a fleet of fifteen English yachts in a fifty-three-mile race around England's Isle of Wight, bringing the Cup to the New York Yacht

Club. Since then, the Cup has been the possession of the last yacht club to win it outright—or defend it against foreign challengers. The Cup began as the province of the wealthy elite—the Vanderbilts and the Liptons. Recently, it has become more a contest of professional career sailors such as Dennis Conner and Paul Cayard than the wealthy men who took up the sport as an avocation, such as Ted Turner and Bill Koch.

Since that victory over the English more than a century ago, the America's Cup remained with the New York Yacht Club—the granddaddy of American yacht clubs, which allowed women to become full-fledged members only eleven years ago—until 1983, when the Australian skipper, John Bertrand, defeated Dennis Conner. Dennis then went Down Under, regained the Cup in 1987, and brought it to his home port in San Diego. In 1992, Bill Koch's boat *America³* defeated Dennis for the right to defend the Cup for the San Diego Yacht Club, and then defeated the Italians in the finals. As a result, the "Auld Mug" had stayed in San Diego, and the yacht club's grand poo-bahs reigned over the event as the extraordinarily powerful Defense Committee in 1995.

Some men from this committee had objected to our team's entry. With Bill Koch as our wealthy patron, we had money, clout, and every right to enter. But when Bill first broached the idea of a women's team to the Defense Committee, they told him we were not "strong or competent enough" to mount a serious defense. The committee did not believe women had what it took to maneuver around the race course in the nearly twenty-ton, seventy-five-foot-long boats with 110-foot masts that scrape the sky. Instead of seriously defending "their" Cup, they thought we would end up as an embarrassment to the sport.

But that didn't happen. At the awards ceremony after our narrow defeat, Defense Committee Chairman Wytie Cable stood on the stage and congratulated all of us for our efforts over the preceding four months of racing. The committee acknowledged the women's team as a positive addition to the Cup for having focused considerable public interest on the event. They also expressed confidence that Dennis had the best U.S. team to duel against the formidable New Zealand team in the upcoming final America's Cup races.

DAWN RILEY

Our team captain, Dawn Riley, then spoke on our behalf. She said that being a part of our team's monumental progress meant more to her than winning did in 1992. That year, Dawn, just twenty-seven years old, broke through the men-only barrier to win a spot on Bill Koch's victorious America[3] team. She was the one woman on our team who had previous America's Cup experience. She had proved she knew how to hold her own among men.

Dawn thanked Bill for his foresight and courage in fielding the first women's team in the America's Cup. We owed our once-in-a-lifetime opportunity to him. Our equipment and technology, design team, and coaching staff were as good as he could put together. Through the nonprofit America[3] Foundation, Bill provided the team with a living wage, two meals a day, and a housing stipend. Bill expressed a personal interest in our success, attended our morning workouts, gave us pep talks, watched our races, and met with us afterward. As a bonus, he frequently invited small groups of sailors to his elegant Point Loma house for dinner.

Before turning the microphone over to Bill, Dawn introduced us individually. For the first time in history, women crowded the stage of an America's Cup award ceremony. Dawn lingered over her descriptions of the character and capability of the women and one man with whom she had faced the challenges of derision, inexperience, and exhausting labor to race head-to-head against the best sailors in the country.

Bill picked up where Dawn left off. He talked about how far the women's team had come in less than a year of training and racing. He said that the sight of Dennis Conner's team cheering as if they had just won the World Series after slipping across the finish line ahead of the women in the final race was evidence that our team had left an indelible impression on America's Cup competition. Quite simply, the women had "scared the hell out of the men," Bill said. From now on, he proudly predicted, because of the efforts of the America³ women's team, female sailors would be included at all levels of competition, judged by their ability, not their gender.

A Different Kind of Guy

Part of what sets Bill apart in the world of yacht racing is that he came to it relatively late in life and then quickly came to love nearly everything the sport has to offer. In 1992, at age fifty-one, Bill arrived at the America's Cup stage only eight years after he had begun amateur racing. His 1992 campaign suffered some of the same scrutiny and ill will from the yachting community that the women experienced three years later. Bill claimed that science, more than the art and skill of sailors, wins the race. To applause from some corners and grumbling from others, he walked away with the sport's crown jewel.

Critics consider him an overindulged misfit in an elegant, venerable sport. Admirers see him as a generous, loyal, and fittingly rebellious soul in a sport steeped in tradition and conformity. It was

almost predictable that, for Round Two, Bill would throw open the doors of the old boys' clubhouse and flagrantly violate the unwritten "no girls allowed" rule.

On a stage crowded with weathered sailors, even Bill's looks set him apart. Well over six feet tall, with a healthy shock of white hair, Bill is exceptionally pale. His broad-shouldered stature contrasts with light blue eyes that blink excessively, a bottom lip that pouts slightly. He wore his trademark Pucci blazer; impeccably classic at first glance but possessing an inner lining featuring a wildly colorful pat-

BILL KOCH

tern on silk. Bill's looks underscore his complex personality—big and soft, powerful and boyish, conservative and flashy.

A native Kansan whose father made a fortune in the oil business, Bill is no stranger by birth or experience to the pedigreed, members-only nature of yachting. He is, nonetheless, looked on as an iconoclast in the elite reaches of the sailing world.

Bill is not so apart from the yachting world that he doesn't share some of its characteristic male world views. Behind a microphone, he frequently surprised our team with a few singular insights. From the beginning he championed our ability to win the America's Cup, and he shed sincere tears over our losses. But part of his standard public speaking introduction went something like: "People ask me, 'Why a women's team?' And I say, 'what middle-aged man wouldn't want to surround himself with twenty-eight beautiful young women?'" The line always got a little chuckle from the crowd. For me, it conjured visions of Hugh Hefner encircled by Playboy bunnies—nowhere near the truth of what I knew our team meant to Bill. Once, speaking at a sponsor's cocktail party, Bill set out to describe some of the differences he had observed between the 1992 men's team and the women's team. Among other things, he said that while the men came to the coaches seeking solutions, the women came into the coaches' office needing a good cry. I remember looking around at the other team members present; we all smiled and tried not to roll our eyes.

But Bill was blessedly prudent as he detailed the women's achievements that afternoon at the yacht club while we celebrated Dennis Conner's victory.

Our year of being a team, dressed in matching shorts, polos, belts, socks, and shoes—or foul weather gear—or blazers and trousers—came to an abrupt end when we stepped down from the awards stage. We each returned to normal lives richer in experience, possessors of better credentials and a broader sense of entitlement and our own possibilities. Along with pictures to show our grandchildren, we carried with us lessons learned from having dared to venture into uncharted waters.

As I looked around the yacht club that evening and tried to measure our impact on the world of sailboat racing, I received confusing signals. Had we dramatically changed the future for women in sailing? Were we to the America's Cup what Geraldine Ferraro was to presidential politics—a small but crucial first step? Or, were we a failed experiment, evidence that given the opportunity, women don't have what it takes to win against men?

Only two other women followed the *Mighty Mary* team onto that sacrosanct yacht club stage. The first was Dennis Conner's wife, Daintry. She smiled adoringly as he thanked her for her support through a difficult campaign. Daintry would go on to be the only woman to sail on a boat in the finals of the 1995 America's Cup. During ESPN's coverage, she could be seen silently hanging on in the stern in the seventeenth-man observer position as Team Dennis Conner lost five straight races, and the America's Cup, to New Zealand.

I'm not sure when the other woman appeared on the stage, or who she was. I just remember looking up and noticing that next to the man who presented us with our hefty Citizen Cup medals, there stood a young woman with a wide smile, long blonde hair, and a very short dress. Undoubtedly, she was merely a decorative part of a long tradition at those ceremonies. No one introduced her, and she did not approach the mike. She just stood by demurely and honored the men from PACT '95 and Team Dennis Conner with their medals.

Invading the Playing Fields

T he women's team entered America's Cup competition one hundred years after Hope Goddard Iselin,
serving as timekeeper aboard *Defender* in 1895, became
the first woman to race in the Cup. In the interim, only six
other women had sailed in the competition. Most
recently, Dawn Riley competed in the 1992 Defender Trials aboard
America³, although she did not sail in the final Cup races. Christy
Steinman Crawford and Dory Vogel each served as backup navigators on one of Dennis Conner's four campaigns in the 1980s. The
last time women raced in the finals was 1937, when Gertie
Vanderbilt and Phyllis Brodie Gordon Sopwith competed against
each other as timekeepers.

America³, the women's team, was part of a larger movement of
women into sailing and sports in general. The number of women
involved in collegiate sailing has steadily risen since the early
1970s. Women's sailing was officially added to the Olympic program
in 1988. Several years later marked the first all-women's entry in the

Whitbread 'Round-the-World Race as well as the first time a woman completed the solo BOC 'Round-the-World Race. The America[3] effort, in fact, was not the first attempt at a women's entry in the America's Cup, but it was the first to get off the ground with successful funding and support.

In a broader context, women have been moving aggressively onto a great many playing fields in record numbers during the last several decades. Since the 1972 passage of Title IX, legislation mandating equal opportunities for girls and women in federally funded institutions, the number of girls participating in high school sports has climbed from three hundred thousand in 1971 to nearly 2.5 million in 1995. The number of women in intercollegiate sports has increased tenfold. In 1972, women made up 15 percent of Olympic participants. In Atlanta in 1996, more than 30 percent of the athletes were female. Women also make up the majority of new participants in leading fitness and athletic activities such as jogging, swimming, and cycling. The increased participation is accompanied by abundant research documenting the positive effects of sports on female health and self-esteem.

That Pioneering Spirit

The initial reaction within the sailing community to America[3]'s women's team, though, underscored just how much remained to be achieved before reaching a semblance of equality in certain sports: "A snowball's chance in hell" was the under-the-breath assessment popular among dockside pundits. On the record, most people were more polite but equally pessimistic. At an early warm-up regatta, five months before the real racing began, the crowd actually applauded in seeming disbelief when

WINNING THE LAST RACE AT THE WORLD CHAMPIONSHIPS, OCTOBER 1994

our team successfully performed the basic maneuver of hoisting a spinnaker.

When we proved that we could slug our way up and down the race course, we surpassed most predictions and inspired thousands of people, especially women. To our fans, in and out of the sailing community, *Mighty Mary* and her crew were uniquely American heroes, true pioneers. Daily faxes, flowers, phone calls, and mail offered unconditional support. If retail sales are an indication of the impact we had on the public imagination, it was powerful. Sales of the women's team gear—everything from T-shirts to chocolate bars bearing our logo—totaled more than $2.5 million. In my own experience, some of the most striking evidence of our range of appeal came when young boys approached me asking for autographs and saying they wanted to be a grinder like me some day.

When we finally surfaced for air, looked around, and realized we had come within a hair's breadth of eliminating Dennis Conner at his own game, I think even some of *us* were surprised. But with every step forward, we came to expect more from ourselves. Ultimately, we did not go as far as we wanted. We did not win. In the end, there were toasts to be made, wounds to be licked, and questions we each asked about how far we had come and what we could have done differently to achieve victory.

When the women's team began training in the summer of 1994, the major obstacles seemed obvious. Dennis Conner, with his wealth of sailing experience, was the behemoth in our path. Being dismissed as a joke or a gimmick was our other greatest potential problem. The America's Cup is an expensive, high-tech sport. In 1995, the average budget per team ranged from $18 million to $20 million. And we needed to be taken seriously to get sponsorship dollars to supplement the seed money and other resources that Bill provided. Funding and credibility barriers had proved disastrous for previous women's attempts at the Cup.

In our arsenal were nearly all the resources that had created a winning team in the 1992 Cup. We had, more or less, the same managers, boat designers, builders, computer gurus, coaches, public-relations teams, weather experts, shore crew, boat maintenance teams, athletic trainers, and office staff that the men's America[3] team had three years before. Add extra training time to make up for our lack of experience, beef up the public relations and fund-raising staffs, plug the women into the program, and presto, victory.

Looking back now, another set of intrinsic obstacles is apparent. Was it unrealistic to expect to produce a winning women's team with a system designed by men for men and run by men? Like women bumping their heads on the proverbial glass ceiling in corporate America, simply substituting female sailors in a men's game did not guarantee success. Similar to working women who find themselves not getting promoted to management positions because they are perceived to lack confidence and leadership capabilities, we were never given control over our program. Nor did we seize control ourselves, even when opportunities arose.

Who's the Boss?

I arrived in San Diego six months after most of the other twenty-eight team members. I had been involved in the initial announcement of the team's formation, decided not to join for personal reasons, and then changed my mind. In December 1994, I went to San Diego with a naive vision of joining a women's team fighting a battle on behalf of all women. I imagined a team propelled by a collective vision of creating opportunities and changing perceptions. That is not what I found.

The instinctual, animal-like sense for who has power in a group is hard to describe, but somehow, without growling, sniffing, butting heads, or revealing bellies, humans know. Even before I knew the difference between windward and leeward, I knew that our male managers and coaches were running the show in San Diego, albeit with the interest of our success at heart. When the men walked into the room, heads turned. When they spoke up in a group, women's voices went silent. They ran the meetings, decided schedules, settled disputes, made final calls on technical issues, and decided who sailed on the race boat—their judgment, above all, was respected and went unquestioned. Two of the most experienced sailors, JJ Isler and Dawn Riley, had proved themselves as leaders within the team, but they held little final authority. We were being coached and led entirely by men who had been born and raised within the very system that we purportedly had set out to change.

As much as the men coaching and managing us fully invested themselves and wanted to teach us everything they knew, it seemed hard for some to believe that we could win, that we could reach the same pinnacle they had. Understandably—it had never happened before.

During one practice, a man from the winning 1992 team, who was occasionally involved in our team's coaching and development, asked one of the women if she seriously believed she would be chosen if they both tried out for the same position in the next Cup. He was familiar with our effort and abilities, but he couldn't quite see us as legitimate competitors. Perhaps more important, I don't think many of the men believed we could get there, in the end, on our own, without a big brother looking over our shoulders and pushing the wheel just a little to starboard or calling for a little more trim on the sails.

Not that the women's team was composed of little-sister types. Within my first few weeks in San Diego, I noticed the armored toughness of some of the women, and it surprised me. I had spent years on teams with women who would spit, grimace, blow mucus, and wring the sweat out of their shirts in the course of a hard workout. The world of international rowing surely has its share of big-talking women. But puffery and physical prowess were only part of the sailing ethos. It seemed to include the diligent maintenance of thick layers of skin over every conceivable soft spot—small talk, no, mirrored sunglasses, yes.

It simply was not a "please-and-thank-you" crowd. The code of honor included getting hammered and hung over and talking about it at length. Under sail, the women swore loudly and a lot. They refused to have Port-a-Potties installed—we hung off the stern as the men did. High-volume burps echoed through the weight room some mornings. The talk seemed to be more of sexual conquests than relationships. During boat speed-testing, huddled together on the rail for hours with little crew work to be done, conversations tended to be humorous, technical, or combative, rarely warm or fuzzy.

During five months of nearly constant contact, I came to know the women individually, and I left with a picture different than my first impression. There were women who didn't drink, some who couldn't wait to see their children at night, some who said "please" even in the middle of a heated race, and one who never, *ever* swore. For world-class weight lifter Stephanie Armitage (aka "The Brick"), "darn" had emotion. But my overwhelming first impression was of a bunch of sharp-elbowed old salts.

While the culture felt intimidating, it also was liberating. During my first week, I felt oddly refreshed listening to several sailors loudly discuss the details of menstruation as embarrassed male coaches, trapped on the boat during a lunch break, squirmed. The conversation seemed a long overdue payback for the times I sat uncomfortably with my brother and his friends while they compared their flatulence. As much as anything, the women's crustiness struck me as promising. They were real sailors, and as far as I could tell, they had more than enough of what it took to piss with the big dogs.

We're Girls, Damn It

Surprisingly, the women of America[3] referred to themselves as "girls." The word—usually found loathsome in female circles—broadsided me as soon as I arrived in San Diego. The signs all over the compound, the logo on our gear, and the voluminous literature about our team all said "women," but "girls" was regular parlance among the team and coaches. Like "balls to the wall" and "no worries, mate," "girls" was just part of the sailing lexicon within and well beyond our sequestered compound. To most of the sailors, the word seemed to imply youthful strength and vigor rather than a put-down. Early in the campaign, America[3] President Vincent Moeyersoms said, he put the question to the team, "What do you want to be called here?" and the answer was "girls." In a discussion about the subject, in fact, one thirty-two-year-old team member said, "I hate it when people call me 'woman.' It's an insult." She wanted to be taken seriously, *and* she wanted to be called "girl."

I couldn't help but eschew the word. Especially when I heard men on our boats using it disparagingly to one another: "Don't be such a girl, put some more muscle behind that man." "Girl" was better than "pussy," but not exactly a compliment. Like "B.N." or "boat nigger," a term freely thrown around in the yachting world to mean boat hand, "girl" jarred me every time I heard it.

In much the same way that we advertised ourselves as women but viewed ourselves as girls, there was a deeper conflict between our public identity and our own sense of ourselves. Paradoxically, the public image of our team as revolutionary—our hook—was framed entirely by the fact that we were women, but internally our identity shifted away from that perception. Inside the compound's barbed wire, we were "just another sailing team." I frequently heard that phrase in conversation among my teammates and occasionally read it in interviews with them. The majority of the team did not embrace the publicly popular image that we were fighting a battle on behalf of women. "I hate it when I hear that girls team stuff," Merritt Carey, who worked with the sails on the bow and below deck in the "sewer," told one reporter. "The focus here is sailing, not women's liberation. We're an America's Cup team. That's the only standard we should be measured against." The team appreciated "that it would be really huge if we won," primarily because we were a women's team, but at the same time, the sailors were tired of the "whole women's thing."

THE CUP

The sentiment was: We want our challenge to be threatening. We were competitors out to win, not to make a statement. Rooted in the maddeningly sexist sailing culture was the sense that the "I am woman, hear me roar" routine would not be taken seriously. The feminist mantle carried no cachet within the world of the America's Cup, partly because women are generally not taken seriously, and partly because winning, not talk, is what counts.

Most of the women on the team had grown up in the hairy-chested world of yachting. Nearly everyone had stories to tell about having tillers or lines grabbed out of their hands, doors closed in their faces. JJ Isler, a world champion and Olympic medalist, raised with many opportunities within the privileged world of the San Diego Yacht Club, said she always had religiously followed the America's Cup, but she never thought that *she* could race on that hallowed course.

Sailing's dominant perspective—the one a sailor almost had to adopt in order to be successful—saw women's events and women's teams as second-class. Many of the women had honed their sailing skills hoping to be good enough to get *off* of women's boats and *on* to men's boats. Some of the women, in fact, said they initially had reservations about joining the women's team because they weren't sure how they would get along with a group of women after sailing on boats with men for so long. Linda Lindquist, who split her time between sailing with the team and marketing, said after the campaign: "I had spent my whole life working with and competing against men. I was worried that the intensity of a group of inexperienced women would not be high enough." Although we had Olympic medalists, a world champion, Whitbread racers, and Yachtswomen of the Year, the sailors' greatest sources of pride and mutual respect were races sailed with and against men.

Our day-in, day-out focus was sailing, not changing the world. We capitalized on the public appeal of our pioneering, female image, but we were recruited for our athleticism, not our political consciousness. The team worked tirelessly learning, practicing, and racing. As a whole, we did not embrace what seemed to me our obvious rallying point: that we each had a visceral understanding of how a successful women's team could transform the game, not just prove that women can assimilate into it. "We're athletes, not feminists," was the refrain. If our efforts said something to the world about women, all the better, but the sailors were there to prove something about themselves.

There was no simple, consistent vision of the team's mission. While everyone knew that all the other sailing teams were in San Diego to win, period, our message was a subtly ambiguous combination of rhetoric about the advancement of women and the desire to win. To our fans from within the ranks of sailing and well beyond, we seemed to be, above all, a *women's* team, trailblazers fighting for a cause. Most of the people who saw my gear and stopped me in the street to talk, hundreds of fans who wrote us letters and faxes, and even my family, seemed to share the view that we were winners just for being out there fighting the good fight. They assumed that we were determined to win, but to them, which boat actually crossed the finish line first seemed almost inconsequential. We were proving that women have what it takes. We were changing the world for their daughters.

Bill Koch acknowledged that the campaign's objectives changed over time. At our media debut, before we had begun sailing, Bill emphasized that we would be "breaking down barriers," "creating new opportunities," and "empowering women." He said in the beginning that he expected our team to do "exceptionally well and to generate interest in the sport." But not long into the campaign, "when I saw the quality of the women involved," Bill said, he became convinced that our team could win. In his public statement a year after we began sailing, Bill emphasized how important it was for us to *win* so that "women can sail farther into history."

The more than one hundred people working for America[3] seemed to have greatly varying views about our purpose. Partly because of our large-scale media campaign, our primary goal was, from the beginning, murky. In 1992, America[3] originally closed its doors to the media and the public because Bill's manifesto declared they were there to win, not do interviews. Three years later, we pushed our women's campaign in front of the camera before it was even off the ground.

Serving a Purpose

Were we first and foremost a women's team committed to changing women's status in the sport and beyond? Was winning at all costs our priority? Were we a gimmick, a public-relations drive for Bill Koch? Were we an easily more tangible means of bringing the America's Cup to more of America, a Bobby Riggs/Billie Jean King attention-grabber? Would we really be winners even if we lost? Nearly everyone had different opinions about those priorities and how they related to each other.

I took to heart Bill Koch's original, well-publicized mission statement. The women's team was an unprecedented opportunity to prove in a large public forum that given a playing field where wits are more important than size and strength, women can compete equally with men, that we can be as aggressive, as competent, and as *good*.

In a system where we were not in charge, and where we were overwhelmed by the chores and details of our climb up the

learning curve, the prevailing focus was on athletic achieve-
ment. I felt that unlike other "barrier-breaking" athletes—black
figure skater Debi Thomas and dog musher Libby Riddles, the
first woman to win the Iditarod—who never set out to become
heroes or icons, we did. We thrust ourselves into the public eye
and became charged with proving something to the world that
went beyond our own personal ambitions.

Even before the campaign began, though, I detected an under-
current of intention to distance the women's team from anything
that could be construed as political or feminist. We wanted to
become a cause célèbre, not stage a revolution. We didn't want to
be viewed as women who insist on being referred to as "Ms."—
unfeminine and unmarketable.

During an early media training session—long before we had
sailed together as a team—I sensed that my vigilance was a bit
askew in the sailing culture. Someone from public relations
raised the issue of language and the media. After a short discussion, the group, women included, decided that the team would
use the traditional sailing terms, such as *helmsman, bowman*,
and *pitman*. Even though we were planning to call our effort
"historic" and "groundbreaking," we would not go so far as to
ask to be referred to as helms*woman* or even helms*person*. The
rationale was that we were out to win a sailboat race, not nit-
pick over language.

I *wanted* to tell the media to say helms*woman* and bow*woman*.
If we were truly out to leave our mark on sailing, the lexicon seemed
a good place to start. Later, when I heard people saying that we were
"just another sailing team," I again felt uncomfortable. I wanted "the
women's team" to be our battle cry, not something we cast aside and

used simply as an advertising jingle. Through all my confusion about halyards, vangs, and bobstays in those first few weeks, I kept looking around for someone who felt the way I did—that if we, the *women* of the women's team, embraced our mission to fight for a new understanding of women, that unity, more than anything else, would fuel us toward victory.

A Team Forms

September 23, 1993

I ran up the stairs to my apartment in my usual graduate-school frenzy. Two stories due the next day, and I had to fit in a run. The night before, after a glass of wine, I had told the wrong person how much "fun" I thought it would be to run the New York City marathon that was coming up in less than two months. "Oh, really," said my friend, a veteran of nearly twenty New York City marathons, "I'll get you an official number."

I unlocked the two deadbolts necessary on any apartment door in my Upper West Side neighborhood. I wasn't certain I could make twenty-six miles, although I had been a competitive athlete since joining the swimming team in Manhattan, Kansas, at age seven. In the year that had passed since I won a bronze medal in rowing at the 1992 Olympics, I hadn't done much serious training. My focus had shifted to figuring out how to live my life without having it defined by a daily routine of eating, sleeping, rowing, and one absolute, overarching goal—an Olympic gold medal.

Sitting on the edge of the futon in my little studio twenty blocks from Columbia University Graduate School of Journalism, I impatiently listened to the messages on my answering machine. "I have to get out the door for a run," I kept thinking. Several people returned calls about stories on which I was working, and I absent-mindedly scribbled down their numbers.

One of the messages pulled me out of my musings. It was a hoax, I was sure. Oh-so-slowly, in not quite a twang, not quite a drawl, a man identified himself as Bill Koch. "I have an idea I would like to talk to you about," he said. Before he hung up, he left his number and added, in case I didn't know, that he was the winner of the last America's Cup.

Of course I knew who Koch was. The name and the family business, Koch Industries, have been big in Kansas for a couple of generations.

Muscle-Driven

Also, my college and Olympic teammate, Alison Townley, and I had watched ESPN coverage of the 1992 Cup and had seen Bill. We had tuned into the then-unfamiliar sport because we knew one of the grinders on the Italian challenger *Il Moro di Venezia*. He had won an Olympic gold medal rowing for Italy in 1988, and was later recruited to be a grinder.

Through the onboard cameras, we caught glimpses of him hunched over a waist-high pedestal topped with what looked like a bicycle crank with handles instead of pedals. He and his partners occasionally wildly turned the handles, sweating, gritting their teeth, gasping for air. Listening to the commentary, we gathered that the handles were mechanically attached to the boat's winches that drew in lines to raise the sails and haul them from side to side.

Grinding was not the only thing that struck me as weird about the sport. The starts, which the commentators called the "high-light" of the racing, were incomprehensible. Guns seemed to go off at random. Two gorgeous boats sailed on a collision course and then suddenly darted into a confined area behind the starting line that seemed much too small for their ensuing game of cat and mouse. Eventually, the sleek vessels crossed the starting line again, often heading in opposite directions and sometimes well after the last gun. While the onboard microphones picked up eerie creaking and grinding, virtually motionless hours passed.

ANNA SEATON HUNTINGTON

We did not understand the action or the subtleties of sailing, but I do remember that Alison and I complained bitterly—if recreationally. We knew several American men who, as in the case of our Italian friend, had also been asked to sail on America's Cup teams as grinders when their Olympic rowing careers were over. "It isn't fair," we griped. We took it for granted that, as women, we would never get a chance to compete in that league. We never dreamed that three years later the two of us, along with my rowing partner of six years, Stephanie Maxwell-Pierson, would be in San Diego with America³.

I waited a day or two before returning Bill Koch's call. First, I called my father in Kansas to find out if he had any idea why Koch might have called. Not a clue. Fully expecting a practical jokester friend on the other end of the line trying to dupe me, I dialed the number. When a child answered the phone and said he would get his dad, I started getting nervous.

In his deliberate way—no shortage of pauses in between statements—Bill delivered his idea. First women's team in the America's Cup. Training and racing in San Diego for a year and a half. Women could win under his program. Fast boats and teamwork more important than strength. Historic. Salary. Wanted some rowers to fill the grinder positions. The U.S. Rowing Association had recommended me. Big secret, do not tell a soul. Was I interested? Someone would get back to me.

All of a sudden, I had a lot more to worry about than getting in shape for the marathon. Bill didn't say it, but I knew that grinders were yachting's beasts of burden. The prospect of the work didn't scare me, but jumping back into the "my body is a machine" mentality did. My identity was just beginning to shift from athlete to writer. I knew I couldn't pass up the opportunity, but would I feel as purposeless when I finished sailing as I had when I finished rowing? Would that anguishing process of "what next" start all over again?

Those questions faded into the background, and my curiosity got the best of me when an airline ticket and invitation arrived asking me to join Bill and a core group of sailors for a media training seminar at his home on Cape Cod. The brief explanation given for the meeting was that the media would be highly interested in a women's team, and we needed to know how to handle the attention.

Six women who were being considered for the team—five world-class sailors and I—gathered with a large group of people from America³ public relations and management for a weekend in one of Bill's enormous waterfront houses in Osterville. Will Robinson, a former television news reporter and a cousin of Bill's who had joined the 1992 America³ campaign to redirect a public-relations effort gone awry, led us through a discussion of the power of the media. He used examples from the 1992 presidential campaign to help us understand how forceful—and at times whimsical—the press is in shaping the public's perception of reality.

To get our message across to the public and to get the attention of potential corporate sponsors, the strategy of the women's team would be to control the media as much as possible. We went over a list of buzz phrases like *historic effort* and *breaking down barriers.* We were taught Koch's formula for winning an America's Cup campaign: 55 percent boat speed, 5 percent luck, 20 percent tactics, and 20 percent crew work. Of the crew work component, strength is only 10 percent and thus ends up representing less than 2 percent of the total equation. Boat speed is overwhelmingly the determining factor in winning. The formula would be a useful weapon against the public's and media's biggest source of doubt—were women strong enough to compete against men? If you didn't like a reporter's question, you simply did not answer it. We had mock news conferences where we were grilled with questions: "Isn't this whole thing just a public relations gimmick for Bill Koch?" "What makes you think women are really tough enough to handle these boats in races against men?"

Sitting at that conference table in a room just down the hall from Bill's big game trophy room filled with huge heads of wild animals that he, his father, and brothers had killed around the world thirty years earlier, I felt disoriented. Sailing, the America's Cup, wealth on such a scale, and public relations-strategies were new to me. I looked hard at everyone in the room, trying to fathom the situation. I could tell right away that Dawn Riley and JJ Isler, the two other women there who eventually ended up on the team, were very different from each other and very different from me, but I liked them. I liked JJ, the small-boat Olympic racer for her high-voltage intellect and her witty humor; Dawn, the big-boat, high-seas, around-the-world racer for her self-assurance, her toughness, and directness. The relentless competitor in me sized them up and thought, "Whatever this America's Cup thing is, I would love to go into battle with these women."

If we were initially trained to be on the defense against the media, it was because Bill had suffered from hostile coverage in 1992. The media were frustrated with America^3's uncooperative policy of shutting out the world so the team could focus on winning. Reporters played up Bill's misfit status in the yachting world. Bill could afford the negative press in 1992, even if it damaged his popularity and perhaps hurt his feelings. He was footing the bill for the nearly $70 million campaign. But in 1995, he actively sought outside sponsors.

We were told from the beginning that the success of the women's team hinged on our media and public appeal. Koch would donate $5 million in seed money and about $25 million in equipment and technology from the 1992 campaign, including two boats, *America³* and *Kanza*, valued at about $3 million each. The remaining part of our projected $20 million operating budget depended on corporate sponsorship and private donations. Attracting public attention would be important.

During the five months between that initial Osterville meeting and the day we publicly announced the women's team, the plans were kept secret. We were instructed to tell no one, although later we all confessed to a few exceptions—parents, husbands. Bill wanted to keep things quiet while he negotiated with the San Diego Yacht Club. If he won the Cup again, Bill wanted to be able to choose the venue for the next race. He wanted to move it from the exceptionally calm, remote waters of San Diego. The committee would not acquiesce, and Bill eventually decided to go ahead despite having lost valuable training time.

During the hush-hush months, we prospective sailors were given false starts on the announcement. Twice we were told "two weeks," and twice it was canceled with no guarantee of rescheduling. Training camp was indefinitely postponed from the beginning of December. I began looking into jobs, thinking graduation might roll around sooner than the women's team could be formed.

Those five months were also marked by the best and the worst experiences of my life. In December, my mom called from her home in Kansas City. Her commanding Danish tone was solemn, wavering. I closed my eyes. Cancer, which we thought had been surgically and radiologically removed in 1991, had spread to her lungs and her bones. Her doctor said he could see many spots on her lungs, "hundreds, maybe thousands." He called it aggressive; he never used the word *terminal.*

Because of my class schedule and my budget, I wasn't able to get home to see my mother much over the next six months. I was lucky to have my friend, Alison Townley, living ten blocks away at the time. She had moved to New York shortly before I started school.

In January, Alison called. A mutual friend, Chris Huntington, another Olympic rower from the 1988 team, was having a party, and he wanted us to come. "I should probably tell you, Anna, that Chris's brother, Stewart, is going to be there," she added.

"I'm not going."

I had met Stewart one night on the dance floor of Club Nashville in Seoul, South Korea, after rowing at the '88 Games. When the competition was over, many athletes headed to the bar district to carouse. I was busy consoling myself. After winning a silver medal at the World Championships the year before and returning most of our eight-woman crew, we thought we had a chance for success. We placed a disappointing sixth.

Stewart—six feet two inches tall, brown hair, watchful, crystalline blue eyes—had come to Korea to see his brother race and to write articles for hometown newspapers about members of the U.S. rowing team. After having rowed in college and on the national team for a year, he was working at a newspaper in Berkeley. He had well-defended opinions about the presidential election. He had witty jokes about the orange tiger, Hodori, the Olympic mascot. And he had a business card, which I had kept in my wallet for years.

But I hadn't seen him in five and a half years, and I did not want to go to the party. Alison, as always, was relentless. "It'll be fun. We can leave early."

Stewart and I were engaged three months later.

The Big Announcement

On March 10, 1994, the eight women chosen to make the announcement of the first-ever women's team in the America's Cup gathered in a Plaza Hotel suite. We were five world-class sailors—Betsy Alison, JJ Isler, Allison Jolly, Linda Lindquist, and Lynn Shore, and three Olympic rowers—Alison Townley, Stephanie Maxwell-Pierson, and I. Dawn Riley could not be present because she was skippering the all-woman Whitbread 'Round-the-World entry, *Heineken*, somewhere off Cape Horn.

A few men who had been key players with America³ in 1992, and who would work for Bill again in 1995, were also at the Plaza. Vincent Moeyersoms was back for his second campaign as America³ president and chief operating officer. A thirty-six-year-old native Belgian, Vincent would oversee all aspects of the campaign, from boat design to coaching to fundraising. Vincent hired thirty-four-year-old James (Kimo) Worthington as head coach for the women's team because he is, by anybody's definition, extremely affable, *and* he has a lifetime of sailing experience, including three America's Cup campaigns. When Kimo, who got his name as a child living in Hawaii, did not make the America³ "A" team in 1992, he showed heroic devotion to Bill's key principle—teamwork. Kimo rallied the other "B" team sailors and regularly stayed until the wee hours of the morning to repair and buff the boat for the next day's race, sacrificing even more time away from his wife, Katy, and their infant son, Parker.

The night before the announcement, we were all given rooms at the Plaza, myself included, even though I lived about twenty

THE ANNOUNCEMENT

blocks away. We wore blue blazers, cream colored slacks and navy flats to appear attractive and teamlike for the cameras. Our outfits were accessorized with navy belts and ivory stockings. No strings of pearls were handed out, as the media mistakenly reported. Over coffee and croissants, we were professionally rouged, powdered, and lipsticked. We even had our eyebrows plucked, several of us for the first time.

I watched the pain and surprise in JJ Isler's blue eyes as the makeup artist expertly removed a few errant hairs from her brow. Some of us mildly protested the makeup because we weren't used to wearing it, but we all complied. For me, the media event bristled with the excitement of the Olympic opening ceremony. Walking into the Plaza ballroom with my two closest friends, Alison and Stephanie, with whom I had marched in two opening ceremonies, heightened my emotions. I was, though, quietly trying to remember if I should talk to reporters about grinding winches or wenches, which tinged the event with a sense of masquerade.

In addition to lining up an impressive pool of sailing talent, the public-relations staff purchased three hours of television satellite time to broadcast the proceedings worldwide, arranged a phone hookup to take questions from across the nation, and served champagne after we had spoken and answered questions.

Bill wanted his team to be noticed.

After the news conference, the new America³ team went outside for photos, and that is when I set foot aboard my first America's Cup yacht. The boat, *Defiant*, a trial boat from the previous America³ campaign, had been trucked into New York City from storage and was parked in front of the Plaza to serve as a backdrop for the announcement. Just beyond the front doors of the luxurious old hotel, the glossy white leviathan with no mast, sails, or lines was propped up in a cradle like a gigantic fish out of water. A group of us—eight prospective sailors and Bill, Vincent Moeyersoms, and three male coaches—gathered on deck for a cluster of photographers standing below. I climbed the stairs pushed up next to the large trademark red and blue eagle decal on the boat's hull. I stepped onto the narrow edge of the boat and down into the carved-out cockpit where there were two chest-high steering wheels and four grinding pedestals. Right away I noticed that the boat had a familiar look. Like the fastest rowing shells, it was pared-down carbon fiber; built explicitly for speed, discomfort implicit.

The announcement was greeted with a surprising level of media interest. Several stories questioned Koch's motives for fielding a women's team, suggesting that his real interests lay in self-promotion, not the advancement of women. But most stories supported the brave and rebellious spirit behind the women's team, even if they expressed skepticism about our chances on the race course.

America³ launched a nationwide call to arms with the announcement. An (800) phone number was published in newspapers across the country soliciting applications from sailors and women accomplished in other sports. Six hundred and eighty-seven women responded to the appeal. Forty-four women, including the original core group, were invited to San Diego for three, one-week-long, on-the-water tryouts.

Sink or Swim

As the coaches and managers gathered a prospective list of team members, they also had to ready the compound in San Diego. The America³ compound was a self-contained, one-block long village that ordered duct tape, copy paper, and aspirin by the gross.

It was no small job. When operational, the fenced-in compound includes a commercial-scale workout room and a high school gym-size loft for repairing sails. In the front, offices for a staff of more than fifty; in the back, docks, cranes, and a virtual airplane hanger to coddle the huge America's Cup boats. The camp had been dormant for three years.

Head Coach Kimo Worthington designed the tryouts with a sink-or-swim principle in mind. Prospective sailors worked hard all day, first in the gym and then in a variety of positions on the boats. "People thought we would put the girls in the classroom for hours and hours and not take them out sailing the first day," Kimo said. "Instead, we showed them the boats, put them on, went sailing, and we were off."

The women were judged by a small panel of coaches according to the criteria used by America[3] in 1992: attitude, teamwork,

PROSPECTIVE TEAM MEMBERS JOG DURING TRYOUTS

and ability. The coaches added sailing experience and physical fitness to their selection standards. Every evening in a debriefing session, the coaches—mostly 1992 team members—rated each woman on a scale of one to ten in each category. "We totaled the points at the end, and basically that was it; the team was chosen," Kimo said. Twenty-four women were selected. The plan was to practice through the year in two boats of sixteen with some positions reserved for coaches.

The team included a college football strength coach, a NASA engineer, and a full-time mother. There was a charter boat captain, a hotel management executive, and a star from the weekly TV show, *American Gladiators.*

Three exceptional sailors, women who had been chosen to be part of the announcement group because of their achievements (two were Olympic gold medalists, one a four-time Rolex Yachtswoman of the Year) didn't make the team. From the outset, we knew that Bill's winning philosophy in 1992 had emphasized teamwork and positive attitude. His 1992 campaign suffered mockery in the media, scorn in some sailing circles, and an internal struggle for control that saw the exit of some high-profile talent. In the end, Bill attributed the 1992 team's success to the overriding principle of teamwork, and it was the primary criteria for selection in 1995. He made an appearance during the women's tryouts, and in pep talks he encouraged prospective sailors to think like team players, not "rock stars," as hotshot sailors are called. He reminded them of one of his favorite mottoes, "There is no ego but the ego of the boat." If applicants demonstrated too much desire for one position or more desire to be chiefs than braves, the coaches weeded them out. "Seeing some really talented women not make the team because their personalities apparently didn't fit made a huge impression," JJ said later.

The team roster was officially announced in early June, and training in San Diego began about ten days later. From the outset, time was at a premium. Preliminary racing in the twenty-ninth America's Cup would begin in mid-January 1995, the finals in mid-May.

A Position of Power

None of the six rowers, one weight lifter, or Gladiator chosen to be grinders had much sailing know-how. Like male rowers and football players on past America's Cup teams, we were chosen for our muscle. We also had to gain a working knowledge of sailing to form the human-powered engine room required to hoist, tack, and jibe sails that can carry as much as six tons of load—the amount of wind power in the rig.

While the sailors could apply their general knowledge of boats to *America³* and *Kanza,* the syndicate's two boats, only Dawn Riley brought with her any depth of knowledge specific to the enormous proportions of America's Cup class yachts. Most of the collegiate and Olympic backgrounds were in small boat racing with crews of one to five people. Communicating and coordinating with sixteen would be a very different game.

Perhaps most important, only JJ brought much experience in international match racing. While much of sailboat racing is fleet racing among groups of boats, the America's Cup is mano-a-mano match racing. The two forms of racing share the same rules and require much of the same technical expertise, but mentally, they are a world apart. In fleet racing, the sailors keep their heads in the boat and focus on squeezing out as much speed as possible. Match racing is a duel—in-your-face combat. In a match race, a sailor has all the same concerns of nursing every component of the boat for speed but must add a full focus on controlling and responding to the opponent.

The twenty-four women (eventually six people were added to the team, and two left) were given less than two weeks to relocate to San Diego. For some, it meant persuading husbands to follow, ending leases, storing belongings, arranging day care, and taking leaves from regular jobs. For others, it meant zipping up their duffels and going on to the next stop in a lifestyle dictated by seasons, boat owners, and race schedules.

Not long after we announced the team in March, before the official tryouts began in June, I decided that I could not go to San Diego. Stewart and I were planning to get married, and my mother was starting cancer treatment. I knew I would be missing a rare opportunity, but I also knew how all-consuming training would be. After a lifetime of athletics, I thought it might be time to move on.

At the Helm of the Team

I n June 1994, Dawn Riley returned to terra firma after seven months of around-the-world racing with eleven other women aboard *Heineken*. By the time she arrived at her mother's house in Michigan, she was late for camp in San Diego.

Dawn, who had also raced with the first all-women's Whitbread team, was called upon four years later to replace the skipper aboard *Heineken* after the crew suffered through leadership problems and a near mutiny. "When I got home," Dawn said, "I was exhausted. I had lost twenty pounds of fat and muscle. I was so tired and stressed on *Heineken,* I didn't eat. In the six months that Barry and I had been engaged, we spent a total of two weeks together."

DAWN RILEY

Having been a member of the America^3 crew in '92, she knew well the rigorous training schedule; and everyone knew that with her experience, she would end up carrying an extra burden. Also, Dawn had found some of the dynamics among the women aboard *Heineken* taxing, and she wasn't sure she was ready to join forces with a whole new group of women. She was tempted by an offer to join a men's team, PACT '95, a third U.S. syndicate, new on the scene and based in Maine.

Although she had second thoughts about joining the women's team, Dawn ultimately couldn't resist signing on. "I knew it would be an incredible learning opportunity," Dawn said, in looking back. "I was sure I'd get to play an important leadership role, which I wasn't guaranteed at PACT." She packed her duffel, gave fiancé Barry McKay—a world-class sailor from New Zealand, where they share a home—a new phone number, and flew to San Diego.

Thirty-years old, five-feet, six-inches tall, 160-pounds of muscle, with long blonde hair and intensely focused green eyes, Dawn has been compared to a Mack truck. She was the one person on the team who, during the endless tedium of carrying bagged sails between the sail racks and the boats every day, single-handedly heaved a spinnaker up onto her shoulders. The rest of the team struggled in pairs to balance the parachute like sails that, at 4,500 square feet, could cover a tennis court and a half. But Dawn braced the unruly cargo with one arm and picked up something else in her free hand—a tool box or a bag with foul-weather gear—and strode at her blistering pace to her destination, briefly pausing along the way to tell the rest of us what still needed to be done. Dawn's toughness, endless common sense, and firm principles had been gained over a lifetime of big boat racing, which began when she learned to sail on the Great Lakes as a child growing up near Detroit.

I saw another side of Dawn on a joint trip to the doctor when, midway through the campaign, she had a double wrist injury and I had the flu. She marched into the waiting room, several paces ahead, and briefly scanned the selection of magazines. Dawn passed up things like *Yachting World* and *Sail* and grabbed *House Beautiful.* "Kitchens and bathrooms?" she exclaimed, "I love kitchens and bathrooms!" I couldn't help but laugh at her big, dimpled smile as she plopped into a chair and started flipping through the pages. Such enthusiasm for anything household struck me as funny but understandable coming from a woman who had spent most of her adult life devoted to sailing and living out of a duffel bag.

Apart from home decorating, the only other soft spot I ever detected in Dawn was for her fiancé, Barry. The two of them were too busy racing around the world, chasing after the America's Cup, and setting circumnavigational speed records to set a wedding date. But Dawn always wore her engagement ring, even though it was considered a hazard in her work with lines and winches. And on the rare occasions when Barry came to town, I was astounded to see this demon of efficiency and productivity actually waste thirty seconds in the locker room brushing her hair and washing the salt off her face before she walked out the door at night.

Sharp and Assertive

JJ Isler had more or less grown up in the San Diego Yacht Club. She fell in love with sailing and racing before the age of ten. Her parents, Tom and Jane Fetter, owned a boatyard in San Diego, and her father once served as commodore of the club. When Bill Koch offered JJ what she always described as a "once in a lifetime opportunity," she was thirty years old, pregnant with her first child, and living next door to her parents in San Diego's upscale enclave, La Jolla. JJ had recently finished a full-time Olympic campaign in the two-person 470 class. She and her partner, Pamela Healy, won a bronze medal for the United States in the '92 Barcelona Games. She knew the demanding America's Cup training schedule because she had gone to Australia with her husband, Peter, in 1987 when he competed as navigator aboard Conner's successful *Stars and Stripes*. A lifelong America's Cup fan, JJ had no doubts about wanting to join the race as a player. Her biggest challenge would be leaving her baby, Marly, who was eight months old in June, 1994, when JJ began the ten-to-twelve-hour days of training.

JJ met her husband at Yale, where he occasionally coached the sailing team. Peter was initially in charge of managing our *Mighty Mary* team, but long before the team was officially announced, he and Bill Koch parted company. Peter had wanted to designate JJ the skipper, but Bill didn't want a skipper on our boat, and he didn't want any positions designated in advance. Instead of working with our team, Peter ended up at ESPN doing coverage of the America's Cup preparation and racing.

If Dawn Riley was the long-haul Mack truck among us, JJ was the feisty, high-pitched Formula 1 car. The physical resemblance between Dawn and JJ ends with their blonde hair and direct gazes. Lanky and brainy, JJ would have been flattened if she had tried Dawn's routine of single-handedly picking up a spinnaker. But, there is nothing fragile about JJ's personality. At Yale, JJ was the first

JJ ISLER

woman named captain of the coed sailing team. She skippered her boat in the Olympics, then went on to become the first female skipper on the elite international match racing circuit. In her position behind the wheel for starts, and while standing beside driver Leslie Egnot calling tactics up and down the course, JJ was an analytical, aggressive racer. Assertive and articulate, JJ naturally took charge during most of our group discussions on and off the boat. Usually, she alone defended the crew's performance to the coaches when we had our group debriefings in the evenings after races and practices.

JJ's intensity is balanced with a reliable sense of humor. At the Plaza Hotel announcement, when we were supposed to be giving reporters the hard sell about our strength and capability in a man's sport, JJ told them she was planning to ask Bill when the "team

furs" would be issued. Looking at us decked out in expensively tai-
lored, matching nautical wear, the media weren't sure whether to
take her seriously.

JJ also has an unusually thoughtful side. One afternoon on the
tow-in from the bay to our compound, I was finishing *The Great
Gatsby*. JJ sat down beside me and asked me to read the last few
pages aloud. It was a startlingly intimate request at a time of the day
when we usually either went into our own little worlds reading or
napping or talked shop in the back of the boat. Right away, JJ
recalled the story, the character, and the themes, and we sat and
enjoyed a few pages of Fitzgerald's mournful eloquence.

The Reserved Leslie

Fewer than three years before they found themselves racing
together for America[3], Leslie Egnot and JJ sailed against each
other in the 1992 Olympics. Leslie won the silver competing for
New Zealand.

Considered among the best Down Under in one of her country's most popular and competitive sports, Leslie was a virtual
unknown in the United States. "What are *you* doing here?" people
asked when she came to try out for the women's team. But Leslie
was born in the United States and raised in New Zealand, and she
had dual citizenship to go with her impressive sailing résumé. She
was well-qualified for the team.

"I came in as an outsider," Leslie explained in her earnest, soft-
spoken Kiwi chime. "No one knew much about my background,
and I didn't really know anyone, except for Dawn." Dawn knew of
Leslie's talents and her dual citizenship from Dawn's travels in New

Zealand sailing circles. Despite her certainty that Leslie would be a prime candidate for helmsperson—the position Dawn dearly wanted for herself—she gave Leslie an early tip on the formation of the team. Dawn also recommended the thirty-one-year-old to the coaches, saying Leslie was the best they could get.

Leslie did not bust down the doors of America[3] to earn a roster spot—that's not her style. At five-feet-seven inches and less than 135 pounds, Leslie had a personality and compact, unimposing physical presence that belied her intensity. When people asked her what she was doing there, she gave them a humble answer about how lucky she was to have a tryout, and then she quickly proved her work ethic in the gym and her sailing talent behind the wheel. "My whole aim when I got there was to stay out of trouble," Leslie said. "I kept my head down, stayed out of the groups and the cliques, and worked hard to prove that I was a team player."

When Leslie made the team, she and her husband, Dave Johnson, had a difficult choice to make. He, too, had just been offered his "dream job," but it was in New Zealand. After a week of anguished discussions, Dave sacrificed his opportunity to come to San Diego to be at his wife's side. He ended up working for the America[3] campaign. Leslie said later she wouldn't have made it through the difficult days of training and racing without him.

Of the five women who were eventually named to the team's afterguard pool—Leslie, Dawn, JJ, and the two navigators, Courtenay Becker-Dey, and Annie Nelson—Leslie was the reserved one. In the gym, where Leslie set an example of quiet diligence, she often came by and gave personal bits of encouragement to people she saw working hard. She went out of her way to make each of the backup B-boat sailors feel a part of the team. In the big group meetings though, Leslie almost always sat silently, her big blue eyes alert beneath long brown bangs. She had to be pressed to give her thoughts and opinions.

The Regimen Never Varied

Each morning, shortly before sunrise, an armada of white Chevrolets emblazoned with America^3 logos pulled up and parked in front of the harbor-side compound. Tanned, sleepy women piled out. Two, three, or four carpooled in each of the cars and vans that were loaned to the campaign by its biggest corporate sponsor, which donated more than $2 million. The women nodded "hello" to each other as they opened the security gate to the fenced-off compound. They shuffled through the gym and into the locker room that they had left only ten or twelve hours earlier. Their tousled, weather-beaten hair was carelessly pulled back into pony-tails—wind-torn, sun-bleached shreds at the tips. Each of the women had hurriedly dressed in whatever America^3 shorts, T-shirts, and sweatshirts were clean in her drawers, or almost clean on her floor.

At precisely 6:30, under the scrutiny of Dick Dent, a former trainer for the San Diego Padres baseball team and the trainer for the 1992 America^3 team, we began a ten-minute warm-up run, which forced awake our bodies for whatever the next ten or twelve hours might bring. The agenda after 9:30 a.m. depended on the weather, whether the boats needed any work or new equipment tested, and later, whether a race was scheduled.

But the morning regimen never varied. Dick, a forty-seven-year-old Vietnam veteran, pushed the team through an hour and a half of stretching, calisthenics, weight lifting, and aerobic exercise. We had thirty minutes to shower, change into sailing gear, pack bags for the day (foul-weather gear, sunblock, an extra sweatshirt, something to read on the tow-out, perhaps a contraband chocolate bar), run down the street to the restaurant that served the team a buffet breakfast, and hustle back to the sail loft for the compound-wide meeting. There, the women sat on the floor in a wide circle while fifty other America³ employees stood just inside the door. First came introductions of any of the regular stream of guests who poured through the compound, including Joan Finney, the former governor of Kansas and personal friend of Bill's, representatives from major sponsors, members of the media, and women from the board of advisers, including model Christie Brinkley and businesswoman Debi (Mrs.) Fields.

Kimo's deep, booming voice then shook the group awake, announcing the "plan for the day." By necessity, sailors are verbally efficient. The sport often requires quick, concise communication—barks more than conversations—and sometimes the habit lingers on land. After a lifetime of sailing, Kimo, six feet tall and sturdily built, was always direct and to the point. On race days, the plan amounted to "If everyone just does her job, we can win," capped with an enthusiastic "Kick their butts," or "Balls to the wall."

These meetings usually concluded with a pep talk from Bill or Vincent Moeyersoms. They rarely included input from the women, although midway through racing, the team began having its own brief powwows immediately after the compound-wide meeting. The most memorable of these featured Diana Klybert. At thirty-six, Diana was the self-described "ancient mariner" of the team, also known as "Dianimal." At the end of the semifinals, when every race became a do-or-die situation, she prepared a prerace talk complete with flip charts imploring us to hone in on our natural, aggressive advantage over all the men: PMS.

After the morning meeting, there was a flurry of preparation— carrying sails, loading lunch coolers and water bottles, rigging the lines on the boats, and removing the dehumidifier and battery charger from below deck. The boats were towed away from the dock through the harbor and out to San Diego Bay, where the sails were hoisted and the long days of practicing or racing began.

Six or seven physically demanding, sun-soaked hours later, we were towed back in. Everything that was loaded on the boats had to come off and be properly stored. If the boats had taken on water, the bilges had to be hand-pumped. Sets of huge plastic skirts were wrapped around the keel and the hull—a tedious and imperfect process that required four or five people and thirty minutes of comic frustration detangling, raising, lowering, discussing, and reraising. The skirts hide the shape of the hull and the keel so the boat can be hoisted out of the water and remain a secret to the competition. If the boats needed work—anything from replacing a mast, which meant pulling the boat ashore and using a crane to lift out the mast, to cleaning or "deyellowing" the bottom of the boat with scrub brushes and chemical solvent—it was done by the sailors and the shore crew. Sometime between 5:00 and 6:30 p.m., the team returned to the sail loft for a video review of the day's practice or race. Most of us returned home an hour or so later; the afterguard or command center personnel often stayed for subsequent meetings.

The Crew Boss

Dawn's boat know-how automatically put her in a position of leadership. On "work days" when the team stayed on land, she assigned jobs and often showed people how to do them. We did whatever needed to be done: wet-sand the bottom of the boat, move several tons of lead into or out of the belly of the boat, take apart and rebuild the winches, and hammer together bookshelves for the compound office building.

On land, it was understood that Dawn was in charge until Kimo or Vincent appeared on the scene. During wet-sanding, for example, the boat was hoisted out of the water, and a group of women huddled around the keel, swabbing it with big sponges of soapy water, and sanding down the new coat of paint until it felt like polished glass. Using finer and finer grades of sandpaper until you get to one gentler than an emery board, wet-sanding creates a keel surface so slippery that the water has nothing to stick to as the boat plows through it. Wet-sanding is part science, part religion. Beliefs about which strokes are best—horizontal, vertical, or diagonal—vary. So do thoughts about grades of sandpaper, to soap or not to soap, and how large an area one should sand at a time. Most of us were wet-sanding rookies, requiring a more experienced eye to check our handiwork and make a call: "Ten more minutes with 180, five minutes with 400 and then a quick minute with 600," or perhaps, "at least five minutes with 220 and then right to 600 for two minutes." Dawn's word was gospel on matters of wet-sanding, but we always waited for Kimo to declare the project finished. And, if in the process he came along with an opinion different than Dawn's about which grade of paper to use, or which part to work on, we immediately deferred to him.

Dawn's years of experience behind the wheel meant that she was trained primarily in that position. Shortly before the trials began, however, it was clear that Leslie, not Dawn, would be at the helm. No official crew was announced, but when we went to check the daily crew lists in the mornings after Kimo posted them, Leslie was almost always driving the A-boat, Dawn, the B-boat.

Dawn felt bitterly discouraged when she was moved off the helm of the race boat, and her commitment to the team briefly faltered. She was clearly one of the team's natural leaders. As she described herself, "I gravitate—or pound my way, however you want to say it—to leadership positions." If she didn't drive, she would not have a position in the afterguard, the command center at the back of the boat. Following some negotiation, Dawn accepted the coaches' decision to name her "crew boss," thereby creating a fourth member of the afterguard. They moved her to the position she had held in 1992 at the edge of the cockpit just behind the mast, called "the pit."

The pit holds the lines and winches that raise and lower sails—the only engines on America's Cup boats. The pit is also home of all the lines (advice for the uninitiated: Never, ever call them "ropes") that control the spinnaker pole. Part of Dawn's role in the pit was something like that of an old-fashioned telephone operator. During mark roundings, she quickly responded to calls from the back of the boat by connecting lines to winches for sails to be hoisted and then released for sails to come down. Perhaps more importantly, because she was one of the few people on the boat who understood all sixteen crew positions, Dawn was officially in charge of "putting out fires." While performing her tasks in the pit, Dawn kept an eye on the big picture. Especially during mark roundings, Dawn helped orchestrate the whole crew, anticipated problems, and flew around trying to solve them.

"Rounding the mark," when the crew maneuvers the boat 180 degrees around one of the race course buoys, is one of the most challenging parts of any sailboat race—and one that we practiced often. There were essentially two buoys on the America's Cup course in 1995: the windward mark and the leeward mark. The marks were big, orange, inflated tetrahedrons placed about three miles apart in line with the wind direction. The race boats went head-to-head three times up and down the course for a total of 18.55 miles. An average race spanned about three hours.

Getting a boat around those buoys can feel like a sustained brush with disaster. During mark roundings, all sixteen people on the boat scramble to get the old sails quickly down the hatch instead of over the side and to get the new sails up and effectively full of wind. Theoretically, roundings are a tightly choreographed dance. In reality, the groaning of the boat as it turns, the spray up over the sides as the hull cuts sharply through the water, the frenzied flapping of sails as they are hoisted and brought down, the yelling of orders above all that, the inevitable swearing and mass of accumulated sail and lines, the intense physical effort, and the knowledge that aggressive precision is crucial, just don't add up to *Swan Lake*.

Not Quite the Skipper

JJ's match racing experience, her sharp, logical mind, and her competitive spirit made her a natural choice for the position of tactician. She was the only woman trained in earnest for the position, which includes driving the boat during the tactics-rich prestarts and then standing beside the driver and trying to outsmart the other crew up and down the open course. "From the beginning, we knew she was the best person for the job," Kimo said. He believed she was the one woman who could handle driving during the high-pressure prestarts. Bill added, "JJ was the only woman who was willing to assert herself in the role of tactician—the only woman who exerted some kind of leadership when decisions needed to be made."

Even though JJ seemed to be the logical choice for tactician, Bill instructed the coaches not to designate anyone to the A-team until the end of preliminary racing. From the beginning of the campaign, he wanted the coaches to train at least two people for each position and to keep them biting at each other's heels. America³ had delayed final crew selection until just days before the finals in 1992, and Bill thought the system had kept the whole team intensely competitive as well as ensuring solid backups for every position.

Kimo's philosophy about crew selection was different. He believed in designating an A-team early. That way, coaching and training energy can be focused on a small group, and the crew has more time to gel and develop. Since Bill was rarely in San Diego during the first half of the campaign, and Kimo was in charge of day-to-day sailing operations, the selection process ended up somewhere in between their opposing philosophies. The coaches did not state that JJ would be the tactician, just as Leslie's position at the helm was not formally announced until well into the trials. But early on, when a backup tactician wasn't trained, it became obvious that the tactician post would be JJ's.

In the position, JJ emerged as one of the team's primary leaders. During prestarts, space and time constraints leave no time for talk and decision-making among the afterguard, so the tactician takes the wheel, and the crew puts its fate in her hands. JJ proved herself in practice starts against the coaches and the other sailors, when the tactician has to think strategy and drive at the same time. "She had balls," explained backup navigator, Annie Nelson. "JJ was willing to stick that boat in places and take risks that scared the rest of us. We all respected her for her guts."

The prestart begins with a multimillion-dollar game of chicken in which the boats sail directly toward each other parallel to the starting line. Just before a possible collision, the two boats turn sharply into the prestart area. A five-minute, sophisticated round of chase and bluff begins, complete with impossibly tight turns and close calls. It's dictated mainly by the nerve and wit of the drivers and a complex tome of right-of-way rules. The object is to force your opponent away from the starting line so that when the gun goes off he is well behind you, or to force him away from the side of the line that promises to have better wind up the course, or both.

As soon as the boat crossed the starting line, JJ turned the wheel over to Leslie, and concentrated on her role as tactician. Leslie, in concert with the three sail trimmers, focused on getting the boat going as fast as possible by feeling for the boat's every nerve and reacting to the waves and the wind. The tactician's role is somewhere between those of an architect and a field general—JJ's main concern was thinking about where to put the boat on the course. Factoring in wind and location information from the navigator, feedback from the foredeck crew, and her strategy, she decided when to tack and jibe, when to put sails up and take them down.

Although JJ generally seemed to be in charge on the boat, and she was the team's strongest voice of command during racing and in our group meetings, her authority was limited. Bill's plan from the beginning was for our team to sail without a skipper.

The autocratic position of skipper evolved through centuries of maritime tradition, partly because emergencies and moment-to-moment maneuvers require quick, decisive action and one clear voice of authority. "On a sailboat," as Dawn Riley explained it, "the pyramid style of leadership, with one person at the top, works best. Look at the navy. There's a commanding officer, and no questions are asked. Not having a skipper leaves things open to committee." Traditionally, on America's Cup boats, the skipper drives and concentrates on boat speed, yielding the decision-making to the tactician *with* the caveat that the skipper, with the wheel, can override.

In 1992, America³ broke tradition. Bill was the skipper, tactician David Dellenbaugh was second in command, and helmsman Buddy Melges, third. Our team moved even further away from tradition—there was no chain of command; we were to work together and share leadership. Ours was the only America's Cup team to enter the trials without a skipper. Bill's thinking in 1995 was based on the fact that the 1992 America³ campaign had suffered through intense battles for power and authority, including an attempted mutiny. "There were a lot of people trying to be the dominant bull," Bill explained. Some long-standing friendships were severed, and a few people ended up leaving the camp. The experience led Bill to eliminate the skipper position on our team in an effort to avoid power struggles among the women.

By virtue of her outgoing personality, experience, and decision-making role, JJ was the closest we had to a skipper. Leslie, with the wheel in her hands, would have been the logical, traditional person for the job, but she rarely asserted herself as a vocal leader on the team, and the role seemed to fall to JJ. Dawn, the other outspoken, internationally experienced skipper among us, was not in contention for the position because of her placement in the pit. Although JJ often acted like our skipper, she was never appointed to the position. As a result, when the coaches were on the boat, they were in charge. When the boat was racing, JJ's judgment was implicitly left open to question, her split-second decisions could evolve into five-minute disagreements, and she couldn't automatically thwart what might otherwise be seen as insubordination.

Instead of hierarchy, our ideology stressed teamwork, essential when sixteen people must function in trusting unison. In many ways, the decision that the women would work by consensus without a skipper fit well with the teamwork principle. Some of the women prided themselves on not having a skipper. It seemed consistent with the revolutionary spirit behind our team. On the other hand, some of the more experienced sailors considered it an odd decision but believed that it was Bill's to make.

Kimo liked the no-skipper concept because he did not want to burden one woman with too much responsibility. "It's too big of a job," Kimo said. "If we made one person skipper, in charge of x, y, and z all the time, something would have slipped." Kimo said that designating one woman skipper would have overtaxed an America's Cup novice. "We wanted one of the women to lead, but making one of them skipper wasn't realistic," he said. Kimo acknowledged that, by default, not designating a woman skipper meant more responsibility and authority remained in his hands.

Having teamwork as our overriding principle and eliminating the skipper's position meant that sailors cautiously asserted their individual wills. Women with good credentials had been cut from the team because it appeared they were more intent on being stars than team players. Even months before selection, it was understood that egos should be kept in check. During an early MTV promotional spot filmed aboard a boat at the San Diego Yacht Club and featuring a handful of America[3] hopefuls, JJ repeatedly scooted away from the wheel of the boat. I made a comment, and JJ laughed at herself. She whispered that she didn't want Bill to think she wasn't a team player, or that she saw herself only in the back of the boat—with the afterguard.

In theory, not having a skipper meant that different people were in charge at different times. On shore, before and after sailing and during work days, the pecking order was clear: Dawn was like a middle manager between the team and Kimo and Vincent. During starts, JJ was skipper. But when the boat was racing on the open course, and the coaches were out of range, there was no clear boss, although there were many important decisions to be made quickly and under pressure. JJ had been told to call the shots; according to Bill, "She had been given total tactical control." But JJ

KIMO, LEFT, AND VINCENT

hadn't been given a skipper's carte blanche. Her decisions were always subject to the coaches' question. And the teamwork principle called for cooperation with crew members who questioned her calls, not authoritarian control. "It was never cut and dried," JJ said. "I never felt that I had been given real control. And you didn't want to be seen trying to grab power. No one's position was guaranteed. It left a lot of things vague on the race course."

A Youthful Crew

The America[3] program did not foster team leadership, and there was no "old guard" among us to assume the leadership mantle naturally—or to wrestle it out of the coaches' hands. Our roster included women who were experienced sailors for their age, but the average age of our afterguard, our leadership corps, was thirty. In contrast, on average, Conner's afterguard had more than ten years on us. The 1992 America³ afterguard was an average of twenty years older than ours—the older guys were the "brains" in the back of the boat while the younger guys handled the more physical positions in the front.

Sailing, unlike many other sports, allows for people to get better as they get older, especially on big boats where the duties are specialized, and a few key positions, such as tactician and navigator, require very little physical effort. Older, experienced female racers exist, but only three applied to America³, and none was chosen to be sailor or coach. Looking back, Bill said he regrets not including older women in the leadership of the program. "Vincent suggested early on that we should get some women for management positions, but we didn't know any with experience, so we decided to go with what had worked in the past. If we'd had senior women involved in the program, they would have known what the problems are in managing and leading women versus men."

One such senior woman, fifty-six-year-old Barbara Farquhar, eventually entered the America³ circle. A Massachusetts native, she has a lifetime of sailing and racing experience. Barbara is one of four women out of ninety people certified by the International Yacht Racing Union as an International Umpire. She was asked to serve as an America's Cup umpire, following the races in motorboats and deciding protests on the water. After being assigned to work with America³ for a week shortly before the racing began, Barbara said, she was "so impressed and so excited about the women's team" that she lobbied Kimo to come on as a rules coach. Coming in late, Barbara was not in a position to do much more than teach the afterguard the nitty-gritty of rules and umpiring. "The timing of my arrival," Barbara said after the campaign, "made it awkward for me to assert myself. I sensed that I posed a threat to the other coaches."

I couldn't help but wonder later what sort of influence Barbara, or a few other women of her stature, would have had on the team if she had been with us from the beginning, either as a sailor or a coach. When Barbara walked into the room, all of us stood up a little straighter. Barbara's short, graying hair always looked perfect, even after a full day of riding in chase boats or after an all-nighter negotiating race committee rulings. Her foul-weather gear appeared miraculously spotless. Her proper New England manner and her extensive experience commanded respect. Thrown into the mix of our team from the beginning, Barbara could have provided leadership and maturity as well as been a natural equalizer with the coaches.

The relative youthfulness of our team may have been due in part to the fact that our coaches were young. Kimo and his assistant, Stu Argo, were younger than thirty-five. According to Bill, "the coaches had a bias toward younger women." It was the coaches, Bill said, who added physical fitness to his original selection criteria of teamwork, attitude, and talent. And, as Kimo explained, "Sailors much older than thirty-five were almost automatically ruled out because of the fitness program." I had to wonder if the coaches had apprehensions about older women meeting their standards for cooperation as well. It may have been coincidence, or another indication of the coaches' affinity for younger sailors, that the average age on the race boat was twenty-seven, while on the B-boat it was thirty-two.

Our team did not worry that we were young compared with our competition, nor did we worry that we had no older women among us to take charge naturally. Teamwork and physical fitness were part of our official program. Leadership and maturity weren't. Most of us, like our coaches, assumed that older women would not have been able to handle the physical demands of our schedule that kept us all exhausted. Working out together for an hour and a half every day before getting down to the real work on the boats did a lot for our team bonding and for each person's self-confidence. Several times when I was running with a group of people, we passed Dennis Conner on his leisurely morning walk to the coffee shop or on his way back, doughnut and coffee in hand, and we took satisfaction in our superior regimen.

Learning to Tack and Jibe

Shortly after our wedding, Stewart and I decided that, with five and a half months of the campaign gone and about six to go, we would try to bear the stress that my joining the team would put on our marriage. Reading the news stories and talking on the phone to my rowing partner, Stephanie Maxwell-Pierson, had me antsy. When I told my mother that I wasn't joining the team, in part so that I could spend time with her, she told me, "You're making the biggest mistake of your life." I couldn't resist the opportunity to experience another sport at its pinnacle. Also, I rationalized, I could leave richer as a writer. Kimo had told me months before that he would "leave the door open" for me. (I was given special treatment, I'm sure, mainly because Bill had a soft spot for a fellow Kansan.) When I called him in November, Kimo was to-the-point as ever. "Can you get down here tomorrow?" he asked.

By the time I arrived in San Diego, the women's team was almost fully formed. After months of sailing with men aboard, the women were sailing *America³*—the winning boat left over from the 1992 campaign—"just girls." Team members handled all sixteen crew positions, while coaches jumped on the boat only to supervise. Other team members and male coaches sailed sparring partner *Kanza*. Our new boat, *Mighty Mary,* was due to arrive soon. The women knew whom they liked and whom they tolerated. They had weight-lifting partners, nicknames, apartments, and roommates. They knew which were the good sandwiches in the lunch coolers. Their husbands made golf dates, and, putting dinner on the table for their wives' late evening arrivals, they joked about their "recipe club."

The five other rowers, most of whom I'd known and trained with for years, had become real sailors. As they learned to tack and jibe, they had picked up a little sailor swagger and a phrase or two from Down Under—"No worries, mate." During five months and hundreds of hours of practice, they had gained a fundamental understanding of sailing and knew their jobs on the boats almost perfectly. Observing the blossoming of my old friend Stephanie was a revealing measure of the team's progress. When she arrived in San Diego, she knew as little about sailing as I did, but by December she moved competently through mark roundings, reacted without panic to torn spinnakers, and she acted as if it were perfectly normal to talk about things like laylines and tacking angles.

A New Kind of Teamwork

Major mistakes were behind the team; small refinements lay ahead. A second place finish at the World Championships in October—the team's first real on-the-water test against some of their America's Cup competition—made the America's Cup trophy seem tantalizingly possible. By the time I arrived, the whole camp's focus had shifted from learning and practicing to winning.

I spent my first month in San Diego feeling like a small car trying to merge into a lane of bumper-to-bumper semis going sixty. The exhausting schedule, combined with learning new names and faces, an extensive vocabulary in a technical sport, and the basics of sailing, overwhelmed me. I missed Stewart, who remained at his job with the *San Francisco Examiner*. Initially, I had to concentrate more on staying out of people's way than on figuring out how to make a contribution to the speed of the boat. The role of newcomer in a tightly established group is never pleasant. And as an athlete who's used to feeling integral to a team, the sense that I was superfluous was a source of daily anxiety.

From the day I arrived, I knew that closing the strength and knowledge gap with the other grinders would be difficult. Under the tutelage of John Hufnagle, one of the grinders from the '92 team, I came to understand the feverish, clenched-teeth, sweaty grinding work that I had first seen on television when I had watched the America's Cup three years earlier. During practices, that bloodthirsty feeling, familiar from my days as a collegiate and Olympic rower, started to creep up on me whenever we approached the starting line. I learned anew how to channel my competitive spirit. I threw myself into the early morning workouts. The weight lifting and running were tiring when coupled with ten hours of carrying sails, grinding, and technical learning, but I enjoyed the familiarity of those workouts.

In the midst of adjusting to my life at camp, I managed to wake up at 3:00 A.M. several days in a row to write a story about my initial impressions for *The New York Times*. Among my observations about how tough and salty the group of women seemed to be, I mentioned my discomfort with the use of the word *girls*. I wondered in print if "a bunch of girls can really beat the men? Are all the codes and modes of long-established sailor behavior going to get us over the finish line first, or do we need to define and refine some for ourselves?" I hadn't thought of myself as a girl since I was a college freshman. *Girls* struck me as regressive, a concession to the outdated, chauvinistic way of doing things that we, the women's team, ostensibly wanted to change.

The article proved to be less than a hit with many of my teammates and coaches. I was oblivious to the reaction until Dawn Riley pulled me aside (literally *pulled* me aside by the sleeve of my foul-weather jacket) after practice the Sunday the article ran. "Don't let anybody give you any shit about your article," she warned. Dawn simply told me, "What's important is that you write honestly." Where I expected thought-provoking dialogue with my teammates, I mostly got remonstrations about having no right to be critical of the team. Some of the younger women refused to talk to me for weeks. I had defied the party line, and so, in the prevailing view of my teammates, I had hurt the team. Even some of the rowers with whom I had been friends for years said they were shocked that I had taken the liberty of expressing myself so freely.

Kimo and Vincent expressed concern about the controversy. They worried that I had damaged the team as well as my standing with the group. Vincent asked to see any future articles before publication. Bill Koch liked the article. Several days after it appeared, in an appearance at a prerace meeting, he earnestly told the team: "You are women, not girls. Now go out there and kick those men's butts."

The whole incident left me in a state of shock. Since childhood, coaches and teammates had called me "a strong team player." I trusted those instincts in myself, which by my definition include giving the best of yourself for the good of the team *and* a willingness to be controversial. I wasn't sure if I had unintentionally betrayed the team, or if at America³ teamwork included a greater measure of acquiescence than I was used to.

When I felt myself outside the curve on another issue, I just kept my mouth shut. At a party in July, long before I arrived, team member Annie Nelson dumped her rum and Diet Coke on Dennis Conner's head after he allegedly made a comment about her being on the "lesbo boat." Annie, thirty-five, had known Dennis through San Diego sailing circles for years. She approached Dennis's dinner table at the party hoping for some diplomatic friendliness. When Annie introduced herself to Dennis's wife, Daintry, Dennis objected. He told Daintry not to speak to Annie because she was on "a boat full of lesbians." Their words got heated, and Annie impulsively poured her drink over the seated skipper's head.

ANNIE NELSON

The exchange was, of course, juicy media fodder. Dennis denied having made the comment, but reporters continued asking for our reactions even five months later. We were told by public relations not to feed the fire, that we needed to maintain some goodwill with Dennis. Nearly all the sailors, though, admired Annie for having stood up to Dennis, no matter what he said to her.

I thought it was almost laughable that Dennis pulled out that old "lesbian" chestnut to heave at us. Fifty years before, people tried to dismiss Babe Didrikson's extraordinary athletic talents with the same label. But, once again, I felt off-balance when the subject came up on the boat during a lunch break. One sailor brazenly asked the coach who was aboard, "So what did you think when you realized we were a bunch of raging heterosexuals and not a bunch of dykes?"

As the conversation continued, I realized that people objected to Dennis's statement not simply because he had been dismissive of our program, but because he had called us lesbians. "Doesn't he know," someone asked, "that nearly all of us are married or have boyfriends?" Later I read interviews with team members specifying the number of us who were married or planning to get married. I couldn't help but wonder how we were making things better for women by giving defensive credence to Conner's stupid comment.

Being a B-boat Stalwart

Coming late to the team, I missed the assimilation period in which everyone put aside some of her personal views and goals in the interest of the team. Most of the women of the America[3] organization loved to sail, and that is what they were doing there. Sailing. Period. Only a handful of sailors had come to America[3] hoping to push the door open for other women. Some were looking to gain a whole new set of skills and experience to take with them to another boat in their lives as professional sailors. A few of the women went to San Diego primarily because it presented an opportunity to save money. Some were simply enjoying the intensely competitive experience. Whatever our reasons for being there, everyone's goals depended on winning. We put aside our differences and focused on that simple goal, which was our common ground.

I struggled to prove my commitment to the team and to winning, and I tried to focus solely on the physical aspects of training and on learning the job of grinder. Several days before our first race, Kimo put his arm around me and told me that I wouldn't be rotated onto the race boat during the first round. I wasn't "up to speed." My tears and speechlessness startled me. I knew the decision was perfectly reasonable, and I'd only been in San Diego a month, but I wanted a place, a purpose on the team.

SUSAN DENT BUFFS THE HULL AFTER WET-SANDING THE BOAT

In later rounds, I infrequently rotated onto the race boat, but my job was backup. There were eight of us who ended up B-boat stalwarts, and we bonded. In charge of tuning-up and gathering weather information for the A-team on race days and trying to beat them on practice days, we took on a life of our own. Off the water, we took up slack with sponsors by putting on our blazers and smiles and attending cocktail parties, autograph signings, and sales meetings. Under the guidance of two of the oldest and most charismatic people on the team, Diana Klybert and Annie Nelson, we prided ourselves on being "the ready-to-go boat." If the race boat was "A^3," we were "B-cubed;" if their motto was "teamwork, talent, and technology," ours was "flexible, supportive, and on Valium." We had our pity parties, to be sure. It was the first junior varsity experience of my athletic life, both humbling and painful. But through the end, our boat worked hard hoping to contribute to the team, if not get a shot at the A-boat.

Head-to-Head With Dennis

ill Koch's prerace pep talks are memorable for their variety as well as their conviction. We heard New Age philosophy: Win because we all love each other. We heard tough-love commands: Go out there and prove what you're made of. There were lessons in military history and heartfelt confessions about his overcoming an early "nerd" complex. He passed on good-luck wishes from his young son, Wyatt, and recited Native American wisdom from the plains of Kansas. Wearing our matching navy shorts, white polo shirts, belts, and boatshoes, we sat on the floor of the sail loft looking up at him and whatever the theme, we listened attentively. He had given us all this—the boats, the sails, the gym, the breakfast we'd just eaten, the clothes we were wearing. Over and over, I'd heard it all summed up as "the opportunity of our lifetimes." We sat silent as a church congregation and applauded when he finished.

On January 13, 1995, the morning of our first race, Bill's tone was mischievous. "Dennis Conner rang my doorbell at eleven last night," he told us. Dennis, who lived just down the street from the fashionable water-side house Bill rented during the campaign, had been out for a walk. "I didn't want to let him in because it was so late," Bill said. "But he looked troubled." Bill invited the skipper in for a glass of Montrachet among his Monets and Remingtons. (Bill's art collection, a traveling Louvre that filled a small convoy of trac-

tor trailers, moved with him.) Dennis confided that he was worried about his team's having gotten off to a late start in their training. They were still trying to get comfortable in their new boat. As Bill told it, "Dennis came begging for mercy out on the race course."

Our first face-off against Team Dennis Conner was just three hours away, and we were nervous. Was Dennis really afraid of us? We liked the idea. Rumor had it that the Kiwis had taken a vote. If they had to race the women's team in the finals, they decided, unanimously, to go home instead. Maybe defeat at the hands of

THE FIRST RACE

women promised a special humiliation that scared Dennis.

Despite Dennis's late starting date, *Stars and Stripes* was favored to annihilate us. In their afterguard alone were fifteen America's Cups of experience—ours had zero; together their crew

Mighty Mary in the lead, last race

Boat repairs after practice, from left, Linda Lindquist, Lisa Charles, Stephanie Maxwell-Pierson, Marci Porter, Dawn Riley

JJ Isler, left, with Leslie Egnot

Bill Koch with Leslie

Dawn Riley, left, and Annie Nelson

Annie, Leslie, and JJ , from left, practice a start

Leslie, Kimo, and JJ, from left

Hanna Swett, at the wheel, and Debbie Pettibone trimming the jib

Vincent and Kimo, from left

Jubilant women's team after making the finals

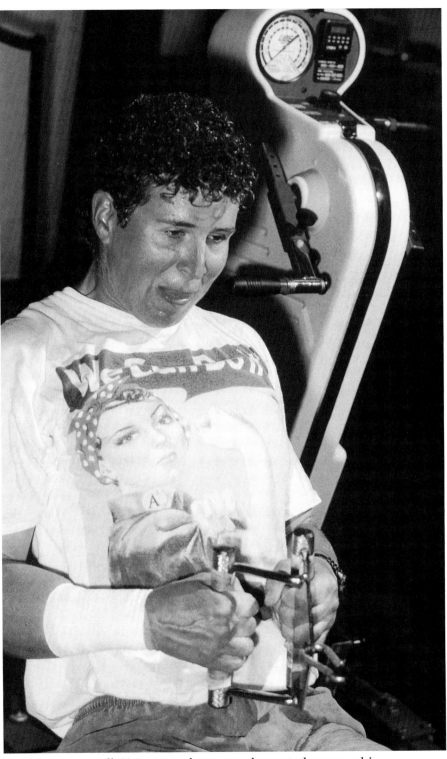

Stephanie Maxwell-Pierson works out on the seated row machine

Carrying sails down to the boat, from front: Amy Baltzell, Christy Evans, Susie Nairn, and Marci Porter

Mighty Mary in action

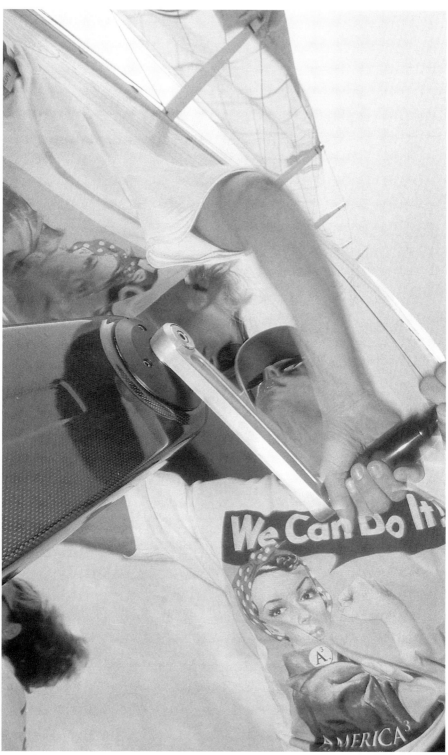

Grinding away

Diana Klybert

Rowing in the gym, Melissa Purdy, left, Amy Fuller, right

Courtenay Becker-Dey, left, and Melissa Purdy, right

America³, top, takes the lead off the start, first race

America³, foreground, duels with *Mighty Mary*, during training

The Women's Team at work

Susie Nairn, left, Meritt Carey, right

Mighty Mary leads *Stars & Stripes*

Bill Koch addressing morning meeting of the team

Mighty Mary

shared thirty-nine America's Cup championships—ours had one. They were in their new boat, *Stars and Stripes*—we were in three-year-old *America³*.

Making Sports History

The story of that first race, which reporters described the next day as "a milestone in sports history"—and to which Dennis Conner jokingly referred as his second-biggest loss, after losing the America's Cup to *Australia II* in 1983—depends on who's telling it. The facts are that JJ Isler, at the helm for the prestart, established a lead right off the starting line. Through the race, Leslie extended the margin, and our team won by 1:09.

How JJ managed to wrangle the lead out of the living legend's practiced hands in the first few minutes of the prestart remains a point of dispute. Dennis termed it a "bad call" on the part of the umpires. We saw JJ, gutsy as hell, rattling the pro.

JJ gained the upper hand through a tactically simple maneuver. She was on port tack and bearing down on Conner, also on port tack. When JJ jibed, she seized right of way from Conner. He failed to steer out of her way, and when she had to alter course to avoid a collision, *America³* protested. The umpires, watching closely from motor boats, ruled in our favor and gave Conner a penalty. Right after the start, Conner did the mandatory 270 degree penalty turn, which cost him at least four boat lengths, control of the best side of the course, and the race. A prestart KO.

That first victory was a moment of intense satisfaction. As soon as the boat crossed the finish line, those of us on the B-boat jumped aboard *America³* to celebrate. The spinnaker was dropped, and Kimo and Vincent brought bottles of champagne aboard. We took out our knives, cut our empty plastic water bottles in half, and toasted victory. As much as we appeared to be saying to the world, "See, we told you we could do it," to ourselves we were whispering, "I can't believe we actually beat Dennis Conner."

The race was the first in the four-month-long trials leading up to the Cup. Hours after it was over, we had to put aside our celebration and start preparing for the next race two days later.

People equate the America's Cup trials, or the first four rounds of racing, to the NFL's preseason or baseball's spring training—as much practice as competition. Teams are known to hold their cards close in the early rounds. The fact that our new boat would not be ready to sail until the last round was considered less a disadvantage than a strategic, keep 'em guessing move. As they had in 1992, Vincent and Bill decided to trade the boat's late arrival for more testing and development time, calculating that we could gain at least thirty seconds over the race course in boat speed.

The lore is rich with teams winning all their preliminary races, looking like favorites, losing in the semis, and going home. So when we lost our next five races of the first round, we chalked it up to experience gained. We felt we had proved our viability as competitors. "Joke" fell by the wayside as a description for our team after we beat Dennis that first day. The question of our physical strength was also put to rest when we proved in tacking duel after tacking duel—one of which included more than forty tacks on the first leg of a race—that the men would have to find some other way around us.

KIMO'S DEBRIEFING

Following our victories, debriefings were short. Champagne always appeared, and Vincent pulled out boxes of Belgian chocolate. Chocolate of any origin was explicitly forbidden by our trainer, Dick Dent. He viewed it as an overloaded source of fat and ultimate energy lows and was impatiently intolerant of what he saw as women's excessive need for the stuff. When we won, chocolate was sneaked aboard for the sake of celebration. When we lost, the debriefing routine was for us to listen as Kimo, referring to his wallet-sized computer, walked us through the race and our mistakes or misfortunes blow-by-blow.

In a nail-biter against Dennis after a string of frustrating losses in the second round, we made a glaring mistake. *Stars and Stripes* was quickly closing *America³'s* lead on an upwind leg. In an effort to match the other boat's acceleration, JJ called for a jib change, one better suited to the building wind. But the maneuver was botched. *Stars and Stripes* saw an opening, slipped over the top of us, and held the lead to the finish.

As we were being towed in after that heartbreaking race, talking among ourselves about what went wrong in the sail change, Kimo, Vincent, and Bill whizzed up next to the boat on a tender. When they jumped aboard, their hostility startled the team.

Bill yelled at us for the first and only time. He swore about our "shitty" racing. Visibly red with anger, Kimo came forward. Few of us had ever seen our coach anything but jovial or concerned, always like a big brother. "We don't have any more answers for you guys," he told us through pursed lips. "You have to come up with some for yourselves. Do it before the boat gets back to the dock."

Vincent said later that the men started fuming while watching the race. "The team was making mistakes they had made before," he remembered. "We felt that under pressure, the team wasn't thinking on its own. There was too much dependency on the coaches. They were always looking to us for answers. We all had the same kind of reaction at that point. They had lost too many races where the other boat came from behind. It got to be too much."

Bill simply said later, "It was time for the coddling to end." He felt that too often the coaches and management shielded the women from criticism and difficult truths.

Palpable shock waves ran through our team as the men disappeared on the tender. We all turned to JJ. She leaned one thin hand against the steering wheel column, uncharacteristically silent. When racing got tense, JJ nervously chewed her bottom lip and played with the Velcro on the pocket of her foul-weather pants while she decided what to do next. The only sound we heard then was the ripping open of the Velcro as JJ repeatedly pulled the tattered flap and resealed it.

"I don't think they had a right to do that," she said quietly, finally, "but we need to come up with a plan." Gradually a discussion began.

Autonomy, a subject that we had never touched on as a group, came up. We had always been mindful of teamwork and its concomitants—obedience and sacrifice. JJ and Dawn led the conversation, which became more animated. Leslie, in her humble, thoughtful way, was quiet during the discussion. Leslie had the respect of everyone on the team. Whenever she spoke up, all of us were attentive, but Leslie was reticent by nature. Dawn and JJ concluded that the coaches had too much control over the team. We talked about how we needed practice making our own decisions, especially in high pressure situations. There were no cries of rebellion, just plans for change. We needed to run our own meetings, our own video sessions. Kimo should keep off the race boat during the morning tow, so that we could formulate our own plans.

As the late afternoon sun set behind us, I talked excitedly with the women around me. We hoped we had come to an important, new beginning.

Privately, JJ felt nervous about taking the team's list of changes into the afterguard meeting that evening. Almost every night, after practices and races, the women from the afterguard—JJ, Dawn, Leslie, Annie, and navigator Courtenay Becker-Dey—met with Kimo and Vincent to go over the day's events. JJ went into the meeting that evening expecting the coaches to balk at our requests for them to back off so that we could practice making decisions. "Those guys had been in control from Day One," JJ said, "and I thought they were going to hate hearing that we wanted to take charge, to take that away from them."

Vincent, on the other hand, said he was hoping for just such a request and then some. "We weren't shocked by the list. We wanted more," he said. "We wanted the women to come and say, 'This is who we picked as our leader.' But they didn't pick a leader for themselves. We expected that to happen in the first two or three weeks of the campaign."

This fundamental misunderstanding in which the team thought that the coaches and management wanted control while the coaches and management thought the team should be taking more control led to a leadership void that haunted the team for the duration of the competition.

A week after our "independence day," it occurred to me that not much had changed, and that most likely not much would. JJ and I were running together the morning after the team had dinner with Lyn Saint James, one of the few accomplished female race car drivers. JJ recounted part of a conversation she'd had with Saint James. The race car driver said she had a lot in common with the women's team. "We are women in male-dominated sports, we rely on sponsorship, and we both have owners." JJ said the last part of the statement struck her—an amateur collegiate and Olympic sailor—as funny. She had never thought of herself as having an "owner."

We did have an owner. Bill spent most of his time away from our camp attending to urgent business in Boston, and in retrospect, he laments not being in direct control of America's Cup operations day-to-day. But, our team perceived him as wielding final authority over everyone whether or not he was with us. Beneath Bill, we had coaches, who in a more hands-on way had been in charge of the team from the beginning. Even after our collective realization on the boat that we needed autonomy to win, our coaches continued to run our meetings, control our schedules, and have the final say. Perhaps most important, their power over us was grounded in the fact that they were in charge of selecting the sailors for the race boat. They posted the crew list every day, and we all checked it. By structure and by habit, we were bound to and dependent upon the coaches' authority.

A Burden for a Pair to Bear

Heading into Round Three, we were still sailing our old boat. We had won only two races. After ten contentious battles on the water, we'd come further than many people predicted, but the team struggled to keep its spirits up.

In meetings, JJ reminded us that most of our races had been close and that we were learning a great deal by having to squeeze speed out of our three-year-old boat. "When we have our new boat, we won't make mistakes, even if we can afford to," JJ reasoned. We all nodded to JJ, but everyone was banking on that new boat being the proverbial "rocket ship." The precedent was set in 1992 when *America³* arrived midway through the trials and proved to be notably faster than the rest of the new breed.

Round Three followed a distressingly familiar pattern. We won our first race and then fell into another losing streak. Once again, tensions started to build, particularly on the race boat between the two people who shouldered most of the responsibility for our results—Leslie at the helm and JJ.

The burden on those two became painfully clear to me during one race in particular. *America³* trailed *Stars and Stripes* heading upwind on a long tack. Stephanie Maxwell-Pierson, my former rowing partner, and I sat beside each other on the deck. Stephanie looked over at me, took a bite of her Powerbar and said, "I hate losing." We had to laugh at ourselves. This was the person with whom for years I shared the principle that when something goes wrong—the boat doesn't feel good, your legs are killing you, the other boat is moving out on you—you just pull harder. In a rowing race in a losing situation, our adrenaline would go into overdrive while we attacked every stoke. Out there on the Pacific, though, we were on a long tack, doing what we were supposed to do—staying low and still in the boat, anticipating the trimmers' calls, looking around for anything out of the ordinary. There was not much that we or very many other people, for that matter, could do to make the boat go faster.

On the other hand, just behind us in the back of the boat, Leslie was transfixed, head slightly cocked, and eyes focused on the headsail, working the helm against the wind and the waves. JJ was looking up and down the course for wind, chewing her lip, pulling on her Velcro, and racking her brains to find some lucky opportunity to capitalize on. The pressure on those two was heightened by the fact that the three U.S. boats were relatively close in speed. Unlike the situation some years in the America's Cup, when one boat has a clear speed advantage and races are characterized by wide margins, JJ and Leslie were often maneuvering through tight, high-pressure situations. When the boats were close together, decisions needed to be made quickly. If the two former Olympic rivals had differences of opinion, the three or four people toward the back of the boat knew it.

When JJ and Leslie had opposing ideas about how close to get to the other boat, exactly when to tack, or which approach to the mark or spinnaker takedown would be best, neither one could pull rank—officially or unofficially. There was no clear chain of command, and neither had any credentials the other didn't have. They were both lifelong sailors, they both had Olympic medals, and they were both new to the America's Cup. JJ, feisty and determined, voiced her opinions. Leslie, stoic, equally determined, and not given to confrontation, clipped out a few words. Sometimes she wouldn't say anything, but her flushed face and furrowed brow hinted at her discomfort.

As Dawn later explained: "JJ and Leslie are two totally different people. Leslie avoids conflict at all cost. JJ thrives on it. This was a problem for JJ because it created frustration between how she wanted to behave, and how she thought she should behave. Leslie could hide behind the teamwork principle, and her sweet, nice ways fit right in. JJ saw all that as weak. She wanted to go in for the kill, but she knew she couldn't because of the teamwork principle."

"I pride myself on being even-tempered," Leslie said. "I hate having conflicts. Under pressure, JJ gets emotional. When mistakes were made, she would yell and scream at the people in the back of the boat. My whole philosophy was to lead by quiet example."

"I was always lobbying for us to be more aggressive on the course," JJ said. "We weren't going to win like they had in '92 by getting out ahead and protecting the lead. None of the three boats had a real speed advantage. I wanted to mix things up, to get in close to the other boats, and sail offensively. Leslie didn't. Her style was to avoid confrontation. She hated it when the boats got close."

The on-board tension was exacerbated because we were racing in an older, slower boat. Regularly, JJ decided against the optimal tactical move because she didn't think the boat was going fast enough to execute it. When she said with frustration, "I'd like to cross them here, but we're not going fast enough," Leslie, whose primary purpose was boat speed, said she could only interpret it as criticism. "I think Leslie hated hearing that information," JJ said, "but what she thought she hated was the style I was giving it in."

Kimo, Vincent, and Bill were aware of the uneasiness between Leslie and JJ. They observed "distracting bickering" when they rode in the seventeenth-man observer position during races, in afterguard meetings, and during practice. They noticed JJ's tightly wound tone and her outspoken opinions. They saw Leslie, less assertive, quietly putting up with it. Vincent and Bill viewed the problem as a lack of leadership and as a "personality conflict." Kimo attributed the conflict to mounting pressure.

Marianne Engle, a clinical psychologist with a specialty in sports psychology, spent a great deal of time working with JJ, Leslie, and the rest of the afterguard. Hired by America[3] a month before racing began, Engle said the focus of her efforts with the afterguard was communication. "JJ and Leslie have two completely different styles," Engle said. "JJ is a verbal processor; Leslie doesn't like to talk, she just likes to feel." When Engle asked JJ and Leslie to describe how they worked with their Olympic 470 partners, she said they gave much different answers. "Leslie said they hardly talked at all. JJ said they talked constantly."

Engle said the situation in the back of the boat was complicated by the fact that when the women verbally asserted themselves, it was interpreted by coaches and managers as "bickering." And because JJ was more vocal, they perceived her as the instigator. As a result, she said, there was a tendency by Kimo and Vincent to "constantly undercut JJ because she was always asserting herself—at the same time, they kept expecting a leader to rise out of Leslie."

Time for a Change

After our second loss in the third round, Vincent made an out-of-the-ordinary appearance at the end of our evening video review. He told us he had decided to make a big change that he felt certain would help us. From now on, Leslie would have the final say on the race boat. He didn't give a reason, and he didn't use the word *skipper*. He asked Leslie if she had anything to say about the change. True to her character, she simply shook her head "no." JJ piped up to explain that giving Leslie more control in tight situations would help by eliminating costly time delays. This was a problem they had been trying to solve in the back of the boat for a long time. Now, instead of having a discussion with JJ about what was best, Leslie could simply make a decision and turn the wheel.

America's Cup boats are so big that many people on the team were unaware of the tension between JJ and Leslie. Even among those who had witnessed their disagreements, there seemed to be little understanding of how this change could be the breakthrough to solve all our problems.

Although JJ presented a brave face to the team that evening, she felt that Vincent had "slapped my hands" and that her position was undermined. "When I went into Vincent's office, he was really pissed off. He told me that I had been relieved of my decision-making responsibilities. It was upsetting. I thought I was doing the job they asked me to do, making decisions and taking control. What could have been a 'let's boost Leslie move' by setting up drills so that in close situations she can decide the right move and build her confidence, turned into a 'let's pound JJ down move.' Vincent's approach blindsided me. I wondered why I was the scapegoat."

Leslie reluctantly stepped up to her new leadership role. She and I packed sails together the next morning. She told me that putting her in charge was a good solution to the problem, but that it would be hard for her. She was not used to playing the outspoken leader, and she was afraid that putting her in control would only cause more strife in the command center in the back of the boat.

Later, Leslie explained that Vincent put her in charge after she had gone into his office to apologize for having argued with JJ on the boat that day. "I had tried to tolerate her criticism and temper for so long. But that day she just pushed me too far, and I stood up to her. I felt so badly because the [former] governor of Kansas was on the boat and saw the whole thing. When I told Vincent about it, he said they had been waiting for me to stand up to JJ and that he would make this change on the boat."

Leslie and JJ spent the next day during practice saying almost nothing to each other. That evening, the afterguard spent extra hours in meetings but made little progress in working out the conflict. They had difficulty agreeing on the source of their problems. JJ thought Leslie needed to be more aggressive behind the wheel, to be more willing to sail combatively. Leslie quietly intimated that JJ needed to be calmer under pressure and less aggressive in her communication.

Leslie said that putting her in charge on the boat did ultimately give her confidence. "I could speak up more because I knew I had gained their [Vincent's and Kimo's] total trust and confidence," she explained. "When it came to tactical situations, I could do what I wanted. You have to be able to override the tactician sometimes." But both Leslie and JJ said that the change did little to ease the tension between them.

The ongoing conflict clearly took a toll on Kimo, who struggled along with the afterguard to find a solution. Several days after Vincent's announcement, Kimo and I had a lighthearted conversation about the situation. He tried to laugh through his exasperation. He said he had been dealing with interpersonal problems among team members all year. He had come up with some creative solutions along the way, but he didn't understand why the women couldn't solve their problems with the same expediency the men had in '92. If a man was out of line, they dumped a cooler full of ice water on him in the bathroom stall. If he was really out of line, they wrapped him in duct tape and strung him up the mast by his feet. The women just seemed to brew and stew.

I laughed at the images. Men and women generally seem to have different standards of locker room etiquette. We had pulled a few gentle locker room pranks over the year, but the picture of a few women sneaking up on another in the bathroom with a cooler of ice water was simply beyond my imagination. Several sailors from our team modestly went into the shower stalls and closed the curtains before undressing, which ruled out the possibility of peering down at one another in the bathroom stalls before unloading a cooler of water. More important, as aggressive as our team could be on the race course or in the weight room, we avoided direct confrontations with each other over the smallest issues. The physical confrontations that Kimo described were off the map—in the locker room or anywhere else. "That sounds great," I said to Kimo, "but women would just never do something like that to each other."

"What the Hell Are
We Doing Out Here?"

Astorm front engulfed San Diego early in the morning of
March 5, 1995. The eight-foot potted palm trees decorating the grounds of our compound blew over and
skittered around like tumbleweeds under the darkened sky. Bill's collection of naked, voluptuous,
couch-size bronze Botero sculptures, talismans in the compound,
looked numb. The gigantic skirted boats, hoisted in their pens for
the night, swung in the wind and pouring rain.

The 1995 America's Cup boat designers built thoroughbreds,
not workhorses. They pushed the limits of fragility for the sake of
speed in the light winds—average eight to ten knots—and the gen-
tly lumpy seas of San Diego. In the tradeoff between sturdiness and
fleetness, the designers created immense structural loads. Most
dramatic were the nearly twenty-ton lead keels slung on slender,
thirteen-foot-long steel fins—watermelons hung from extra-long
toothpicks.

MIGHTY MARY IN THE MARCH 5 RACE

An ominous feeling hung over the compound that March morning. As the team filed into the gym in the morning, drenched during the short, dark walk from our cars, speculation immediately began about whether our race against Dennis Conner would go off. It was the fourth round, and the stakes were high—each race was worth seven points as opposed to one point in the first round. Similar weather had blown in on other mornings and had blown out before the noon starting gun. But when fronts settled in, races were called off.

Our team had raced our new boat, *Mighty Mary,* only twice, and we were still getting familiar with it. Bill named the yacht after his mother, whose athletic prowess, he said, never brought the recognition she had deserved. Initially, the team was less than enthusiastic about the old-fashioned sounding name. During practice one day we came up with a long list of absurd alternatives, including *Castracious, Hairball,* and *Bill's Babes.* But when Bill broke into tears at the boat's christening while telling the story of his mother's hunting and tennis talent, most of us had an immediate change of heart.

Slip-Sliding Away

After hundreds of hours of training and racing, we knew our way around our other boat, *America³*, with our eyes closed. *Mighty Mary* was designed for an easy transition, but small differences, such as the fact that she heeled over more readily and had smaller winches and a different gear-shifting system for the grinders, required adaptation. *Mighty Mary* showed promising speed with a slim margin of loss in her first race and a fifty-six-second victory in her second race, but she handled differently. Leslie and the sail trimmers were working hard to figure out how to squeeze the boat for all its potential.

The memory of *Mighty Mary's* first race—a similarly windy and rainy day—lingered. There wasn't time before that first race to properly install nonskid surfacing and foot braces on the deck of the new boat. The sailors slipped and slid across the wet, heeled-over, polished surface during racing. "We weren't sailing, we were ice skating," was the refrain. The lack of control had taken a toll on everyone's nerves. Nonskid surfacing and footblocks were immediately installed but remained untested in wet, windy conditions.

Adding to discomfort in the new boat was the fact that the pressure on the wheel from *Mighty Mary's* significantly longer rudder nearly lifted Leslie off the deck as she tried to control the helm. She lightheartedly named the extra-long rudder "Johnny Holmes," after the porn star. But her pain behind the wheel became chronic, and she eventually required a neck brace.

The forecast for March 5 was rain all day with sixteen to twenty knots of gusty wind and a four-to-five-foot steep chop on the water. One knot is slightly faster than one mile per hour. The conditions were borderline, but not prohibitive. Generally, in flat seas, more than twenty knots of wind was considered to pose a destructive threat to the boats. In swells and chop, fifteen to sixteen knots usually meant no racing.

The race committee radioed, "The race is on," and Vincent half-jokingly replied, "We'll race if you want us to race, but it's going to be an expensive day." At 9:30 A.M., our two boats were towed out, side-by-side hobbyhorses bobbing through the rough water, dragged on long, thick bow lines behind *Chubasco*. Most of us suppressed genuine surprise when we left the dock. The situation wasn't exactly lambs to the slaughter, but there was a sense that we were taking our new Lamborghini off-road.

On most race days, once the boats were near the race course, we hoisted the mainsails, threw off the tow lines, and hoisted the jibs. The B-boat tuned up the A-boat for about half an hour. It was a standard warm-up procedure: getting a feel for conditions, making sure nothing was malfunctioning, testing repairs, and going through a few maneuvers to get everyone's head in the game.

The electronics aboard *Mighty Mary* were not working properly on the day of the big storm, and so tune-up time went to repairs. The electronics produce readouts on what resemble large digital alarm clocks mounted on the mast and at each of the trimmers' stations. They could be programmed to show whatever the crew needed, including wind speed, wind angle, and boat speed. The information helped us determine which size and weight of sails to use and how efficiently we were sailing. Before the start, the afterguard used the data, along with wind and weather information radioed from other boats stationed around the course, to develop race strategy. Their overriding concern was picking the preferred side of the course, the one they would fight for in the prestart.

The wind wand, the weathervane-like attachment at the top of the mast that collects data for the electronics, seemed to be the source of the problem aboard *Mighty Mary*. Merritt Carey was hoisted 110 feet to the top of the mast with a replacement wind wand strapped to her back. A twenty-five-year-old Brown graduate from Maine, Merritt shared the work on the bow and with the sails below deck in "the sewer" with Susie Nairn. Blotchy, multi-colored bruises spreading from Merritt's ankles to her thighs bore testimony to the challenge of the work and her commitment. Merritt had sailed with Dawn on *Heineken* in the Whitbread 'Round-the-World-Race. She had seen more perilous conditions than these while bobbing at the top of the mast in the middle of the Southern Ocean.

When Merritt finally was lowered onto the deck, she was soaked and even more bruised from her turbulent trip. The wind wand was not causing the electronics problem. The cable that activates the wind reading instruments had been damaged when a new mast was put in the day before.

JJ, Dawn, Leslie, and a few other members of the crew stood in the back of the boat, their foul weather gear already saturated, and tried to decide what to do next. Vincent got on board to supervise, as he did whenever prestart problems arose. Barbara Farquhar, Kimo, Stu, head sailmaker Per Andersen, and shore

MERRITT CAREY

crew manager Peter Grubb stayed nearby in a tender in case their expertise should be required.

The group devised the quickest plan for replacing the cable—hoist three people up the mast, and while they held the long cable in place, connect it to the instruments and tape it directly to the mast. About thirty minutes remained before the eleven-minute warning gun signaling the beginning of the starting sequence. The women considered asking the race committee for an official postponement, but, as JJ put it, "Vincent started directing a game of bluff instead. We could see that *Stars and Stripes* was having trouble with the mainsail. Vincent's thinking, as he shared it with us, was that a postponement would help them more than it would help us, so we should let them apply for it. He figured we could win without electronics, but they couldn't win without a main.

Thrashed and Battered

Team Dennis Conner did ask for a short delay, which was extended to a full forty-five minutes. One of their crew was injured. Ralf Steitz had gone up the mast to correct the mainsail problem, and as *Stars and Stripes* thrashed in the wind and waves, he lost his grip and was flung, like a human tetherball, into the shrouds, the thick metal cables that stabilize the mast side to side.

Shortly before the new starting time, *Mighty Mary's* electronics problem had not been solved, and the project was abandoned. Vincent disembarked onto a tender. With him went extra cargo—bags of dry clothes and the lunch cooler—and all radios except one safety radio reserved for emergencies. The navigational equipment, which allows the crew to know its position on the course, was intact. Despite low visibility from fog and pouring rain, our team could navigate its way around the course.

Just one minute before *Stars and Stripes* was due to enter the prestart area, her crew managed to hoist the main to the top of the mast. The women watched as helmsman Paul Cayard—with whom Dennis traded off at the wheel—struggled to work the barely moving boat into the prestart area on time. When he couldn't, *Stars and Stripes* was assessed a penalty.

Time did not allow for the usual prestart game of cat and mouse between the two crews. The boats simply sailed upwind across the starting line with *Mighty Mary* leading slightly at the gun. Seconds after she crossed the line, the main on *Stars and Stripes* tore loose and crumpled to the deck, effectively putting on the brakes. Team Dennis Conner could do nothing but wave good-bye. Unable to complete their penalty turn immediately after the start, *Stars and Stripes* was assessed another penalty. An inauspicious beginning: two penalties and no main. Their only hope was to limp along behind, waiting for the weather to wreak havoc on *Mighty Mary.*

Stephanie Maxwell-Pierson, permanently positioned in the middle of the boat as the main grinder, said there were different moods at the front and the back of *Mighty Mary* as she headed up that first leg. As *Stars and Stripes* became a speck behind them, Stephanie said, JJ became lighthearted. "She was her typical jokester self. She walked around the boat and told everybody, 'Oh come on you guys, lighten up, of course we're gonna win.' She was trying to alleviate some of the stress from the bad weather, and she knew she could take the afternoon off from a tactical standpoint. All we had to do was get the boat around the course, and we would win." On the other hand, the people at the front of the boat, Dawn particularly, "were all doom and gloom. She kept saying that we needed to stay focused, that anything could happen."

Those of us aboard *America³*, which was handed down to the B-team when *Mighty Mary* arrived, were similarly wary and giddy.

Over the radio, we heard that the injured sailor on *Stars and Stripes* had been bashing around in the rigging for several minutes because the weather made it difficult to bring him down. The news that he didn't know his name when they got him on deck gave us a chill. The high, gusty winds, the pounding waves, the dark skies, and the prickling rain made for thrilling sailing. As we tacked back and forth up to the weather mark, we were working hard enough to stay warm and enjoying the risk of pushing our boat to the limits of its construction. In one puff of wind, we saw 15.6 knots of boat speed, a record in our unofficial log.

Over the spray, no one heard the two, four-inch-wide strips of Velcro that held the reaching struts in place rip open. In our peripheral vision, a few of us saw one of the six-foot-long, five-inch-diameter carbon fiber tubes fly off the deck into the Pacific. Most of us laughed at the calamity; the reaching struts are not crucial. But the sight of the strut floating in the churning, gray water behind us was sobering—what else might hurl off the boat? We made several passes at the strut, and finally snagged it.

Normally, the B-boat stayed out sailing, listening to the play-by-play over the VHF radio, cheering on *Mighty Mary* through mark roundings, and met up with the race boat after the race. On this day, though, Kimo radioed us with orders to take the boat back to the dock immediately. Shortly afterward, we heard over the radio that *oneAustralia* had sunk during its race against one of the New Zealand teams. None of us could believe that a $3 million boat and an America's Cup dream had sunk. In 144 years of America's Cup history, a boat had never gone down; but in the most dramatic display of fragility, *oneAustralia* had split in two and, while her crew jumped off to safety, gone to the bottom of the ocean in a matter of seconds. Our crew was more or less silent after that transmission, the giddiness

ONEAUSTRALIA GOING DOWN

gone. We all focused on our jobs. Let's get our boat home safely, many of us thought, and hope our teammates aren't long behind us.

At the end of the first downwind run, the sailors aboard *Mighty Mary* heard a hollow ripping sound inside the mast. The enormous mainsail slumped and loudly flapped in the wind as it fell to the deck. The lock that connects the halyard to the sail had broken.

"It was almost comical," Stephanie Maxwell-Pierson said. "I worked with the main, so I looked at it a lot. But zip, there it was out of nowhere, in a heap on top of us."

Dawn and Merritt worked on a system to rig a spare main halyard. "Once the main came down, people became worried that maybe Dennis would catch us. We knew that was impossible, but we couldn't see him, so that put a little panic in the air," Stephanie said. In fact, Dennis had given up hope and simply sailed home after the second leg.

Without a main, *Mighty Mary* was a different beast to steer, and Leslie had to fight to control it through the waves. She and JJ began taking turns at the wheel, sparing some wear and tear on Leslie's neck and shoulder. Stephanie said everyone tried to stay positive, but between the wet chill and worrying about the phantom Conner, the sailors asked each other over and over, "What the *hell* are we doing out here?"

A Strange Sound

With the main down and the boat making as few tacks as possible, there was little work for most members of the crew. "Everyone was huddling under the main, trying to stay warm," JJ said. "We tried to joke around to reduce the stress level," Stephanie added, "but you could tell people were nervous. There was a sense that we were pushing the edge. Dawn was especially adamant about telling us not to get too relaxed."

More than halfway up the second beat, when the bow slammed into a huge wave, Dawn heard a noise outside the boat's ordinary creaking and groaning. "It was a sharp cracking instead of a dull thud," Dawn said. "I've heard that sound before—it's not good." The noise sent Dawn scrambling down through the hatch into the dark, inhospitable belly of *Mighty Mary* to look for damage. Dawn found exploded black carbon shreds that used to be a structural rib of the boat's hull. She could see the hull dangerously flexing forward of the damage.

The around-the-world sailor, who once spent half an hour submerged in the roiling Atlantic Ocean tying on *Heineken's* rudder so her crew could make the finish line, stuck her head up through the hatch and yelled to the back of the boat, "BEAR OFF. WE ARE FUCKING OVER."

Stephanie said the grinders and trimmers, many of them still huddled under the main, just stared dumbfounded at Dawn. They had never seen her frazzled, and now she looked frantic. In unison, they turned to JJ for a response.

HANNAH SWETT, FOREGROUND, JJ AT THE WHEEL

JJ, the racer, paused. She had no idea how bad the damage was, and she wasn't sure she could even assess it. She was clean-up crew, not Ms. Fix It. "Dawn has done a lot of survival sailing," Leslie reminded JJ, "if she thinks we should head for home, she knows what she's talking about." "But we're winning," JJ thought to herself. She didn't even want to look down below. She said she was willing to take responsibility for whatever happened. Straining to match Dawn's volume, she yelled back, "Yeah. BUT IT'S SEVEN POINTS."

Looking up through the hatch as the rain beat down on her head, it was Dawn's turn to pause. "Hmmm," she thought to herself, "good point."

Dawn wasn't ready to back off all the way. She hollered that *Mighty Mary* had to take them through the Cup—they had to avoid more damage—she was not disposable like the little dinghies most of the women were used to sailing.

Maybe a Turning Point

JJ just nodded and thought about the seven points the team would win when they finished the race. Those points would put the team back in the running for a high seeding going into the semifinals. The race could be a long-awaited turning point.

The women continued sailing at wide angles to the wind to reduce further stress to the boat. JJ, Leslie, and navigator Courtenay Becker-Dey closely watched the water, calling incoming waves and puffs of wind to be steered around. Dawn and others rigged some temporary stability for the hull.

With the hatch open for the reaching strut, which was now bracing the hull, rain and waves poured into of the boat. Stephanie and the other grinders went below, and, passing up buckets through the hatch, they bailed water. "I was freezing cold," Stephanie said, "none of us was remotely warm or dry anymore. But we stood down there in the water, bailing one of those five-gallon buckets every thirty seconds with more waves coming in constantly. Between thinking about how much I needed to go to the bathroom, I thought, 'my God, what the *hell* are we doing out here?' But, of course, we got through it. And we got our seven points."

When the boat crossed the finish line, Stephanie said, the coaches were concerned. "They pulled up in the orange inflatable tender and told us we could get on *Chubasco*, that some of the guys would take the boat in for us. Yeah, we could hold our own, but we wanted to get off that boat."

As they jumped from *Mighty Mary* to the tender, Kimo told the crew that *oneAustralia* had sunk. Sarah Bergeron, a grinder dating a sailor on *oneAustralia*, burst into tears. The news took a few minutes to permeate Stephanie's frozen senses, but she said it gave some life to the question she had been asking herself all day. JJ, having gotten her seven points, could not be bothered; "Wow, cool, a boat sank."

Woman Overboard

O n the water one day during the last week of practice
before the semifinals, the air was frantically charged
after a quick series of mark roundings. Joan
Touchette, still out of breath from her work on the
foredeck, leaped into the cockpit. "What the *fuck* are
we doing maneuvers for?" she erupted. "It's a fucking waste of
time. We can't even get this thing going faster than the B-boat."
The old and new boats sailed side-by-side in most practices. They
seemed to be moving at alarmingly similar speeds. Joan, a twen-
ty-four-year-old former Coast Guard cadet, was known on the
team for her sailing expertise and her laconic demeanor punctu-
ated by occasional outbursts of frustration. We'd seen her launch
a few winch handles before, but we never had seen this kind of
fury. Her anger opened a valve. Like a pack of dogs triggered by
one bark, we all started griping about how we ought to be using
our practice time and the other things we needed to change.

JJ's voice cut through the din. "Speed tests show we are going much better than the old boat," she said, directing herself first at Joan and then to the group as a whole. "This short course stuff is deceiving, but it's essential work. It's keeping us right on track." JJ's reasoning reined us in, but the fatigue and pressure threatened to unravel us.

We needed to win five of our next eight races to advance to the Citizen Cup finals. In the first four rounds, we had won only five of fifteen races.

"When *Mighty Mary* wasn't the rocket ship that *America³* had been in '92, people started panicking," JJ said later. "In my opinion, the crew handled it much better than management. They were counting on *Mighty Mary* because they didn't have confidence in us against the men in equal boats."

"The pressure was mounting," Vincent said. "Before, we always had the excuse that it's the old boat; we always had the new boat to look forward to. When *Mighty* Mary's speed failed to develop as rapidly as expected through the tuning process, the personality conflicts started to escalate, to show their damaging side." With the semifinals looming, some people, especially Vincent, thought a radical personnel or equipment change was needed in order to avoid elimination.

JJ said Vincent told her privately: "You're not bringing out the best in the boat. You're too opinionated, and you make it hard for people to do their jobs. You have two races to turn this team around. If you can't, you're off the boat." When JJ told Leslie, Courtenay, and Stephanie Maxwell-Pierson about the conversation the next day on the boat, she said: "They looked shocked. It seemed impossible to all of us that they would take me off the boat."

Vincent has a different recollection of the conversation with JJ. "I told her she was behaving like a lot of small-boat sailors tend to do when they are first on big boats as tacticians," Vincent said. "She was trying to make things happen without taking into account the size of the boat and the number of people on the boat. I definitely didn't give her an ultimatum."

In a meeting that week, Vincent instructed a small group of key sailors, including the afterguard and a few trimmers, to think about what they could change to get the boat going faster. He told them to start with a "blank page" and not to rule out any possibility, no matter how radical. "We were pinned up against a wall," Vincent explained. "Asking ourselves, 'What do we do now?'"

Time for a Talk

The semifinals began Saturday, March 18. We faced PACT '95. Before our morning workout, Bill Koch told JJ he needed to talk to her.

David Dellenbaugh's presence in the gym that morning did not seem especially noteworthy. He was among a group of ten men from the winning 1992 team who, along with John Kolius, one of the premier big-boat skippers in the world, periodically rotated through our practices to coach us. Rumors surfaced within the team every so often that the men were being kept ready in the wings should we fail miserably. From the very beginning of the campaign, the men from the '92 team were instrumental in teaching us how to sail and race America's Cup boats. David Dellenbaugh, with his gentle, unimposing style, proven America's Cup competence, and teaching ability, was among the best-liked of the coaches.

Nearly all of us were surprised when Bill called us to the front of the gym—we had come in from our run and had spread out to our various spots for stretching. Wondering what could be important enough to interrupt our workout, we gathered in a tight cluster facing Bill. The walls were covered with faxes, letters, and murals wishing us luck. One letter from a nine-year-old fan told us to, "Kick Butt." Another note said, "Women who seek equality with men lack ambition."

The ever-present, thundering stereo had been turned off. An unfamiliar quiet permeated the gym.

Bill stood beneath the flag over our locker room door that read, "Sail tough or go home," and announced a surprise. He held up a generously sized silk scarf with a pattern of large, interlocking *A*s and *3*s in pastels. The scarves that Pucci designed, just for us, would be in our compound mail boxes that day. As Bill displayed the new scarf by two corners, a few quiet ooh's came from the smiling group.

Then, there was a long, uncomfortable pause. The scarf was put aside, and the smile left Bill's face. "I have been impressed with your racing," he told us, sounding now less like Santa than a boardroom CEO. "But you are not winning enough races to win the America's Cup." No one had ever publicly stated this fact to us as a group. As it registered, our childish glee over the scarves faded. People turned their eyes to the ground.

"Something has to change," he continued. "After a lot of talking with Vincent and four members of the crew, we've realized that this boat has to have some experience if it's going to go all the way to the Cup." Even then, I don't think most of us knew what was coming next.

"I have decided to replace JJ with David Dellenbaugh." Another long pause. He had just spoken to JJ, Bill said, and she said she wanted the best for the team.

Audible gasps rose from the knot of women. Eyes shot from JJ, who, I noticed at that moment, was in tears, to David, who shifted uneasily. JJ took a few steps forward and bravely tried to joke to the team through her tears, "It's OK . . . Bill has already assured me that Dave will not have to shave off his beard." Her voice quit, and she stepped back into the group.

ALMOST A WOMEN'S TEAM

Bill asked if there were any comments. Susan Dent, Dick's thirty-five-year-old wife, and one of the most frank and committed team members, was flushed with emotion. "What about the *women's* team?" she demanded directly to Bill. "What are we supposed to tell people?" She was close to tears. "The whole thing sucks," she exclaimed. Several other people began to cry quietly. No one else dared to speak her opinion, but a few sailors asked all at once about the process of the decision. Whose idea was it? Which team members had represented us in this decision?

Welcome to the Team

Joan Touchette's voice shot above the crowd. "I think we're for-getting something here, guys," she said. The room went silent as we turned our attention to Joan. She squeezed past people to make her way over to David. Joan extended her hand, which he grateful-ly accepted, and said, "Welcome to the team, Dave."

Those five or ten minutes were nearly all the time we had to deal with "the man-on-the-boat thing." A crucial race was just hours away. We had to move past this obstacle, land on our feet, and do whatever it took to win. On the tow-out to the course, there were quiet conversations about the relative value of winning at all costs versus maintaining the integrity of the women's team. "Why did Bill really do it," we asked each other—"because we need expe-rience in the afterguard, or because JJ and Leslie can't get along?" A few of the sailors were heartbroken. Shortly after the decision was made, one of my fellow rower/grinders told me, "I came here because this was a women's team, not because I needed another athletic experience, and now that's gone." She said she seriously considered quitting.

No one did leave the team as a result of the decision. Instead, all of us, even JJ, turned a steadfast face to the public and the media. The team applied the mind-set perfected over ten months of train-ing and racing under public scrutiny—present a united front and move on. Most of us would not express our opinions to the media. Those who did went off the record. Even among ourselves, we decided not to discuss the matter. We had to put it behind us. Bill had made the decision, and our job was to make the best of it.

The understanding that we would be good team players and not foment discussion on the issue meant that most of us were surprised when Bill reconvened us in the sail loft a few days after he announced the crew change. "There's been a lot of talk," he told us, "and I want to put it on the table. If you have concerns, let me hear them."

There were few questions or challenges. We did not ask Bill how the decision to put David on the boat had been made, although few among us knew. The biggest concern was figuring out the party line for the media, which was extremely critical of the "sellout" of the all-women's ideal. "Are we supposed to say *we* made this decision, or should we tell people that Bill made it?" Sailors wanted to know because reporters were asking.

As the conversation continued, many of the women said they felt David improved the team by bringing aboard a new, "calm confidence." This became a much-used description of the difference he made on the boat, around the compound, and in the newspapers. The members of the afterguard—Leslie, Dawn, and Courtenay (David taught Courtenay sailing when she was a young girl in Connecticut)—were more comfortable with their new tactician.

Those three women had played a role in the decision to bring David aboard *Mighty Mary*. They, JJ, and several other members of the crew were involved in a week of tense conversations with upper management, department heads, and outside consultants about how to turn the team around before the semifinals. A variety of crew changes were considered, along with changes to the new boat.

During that week, Vincent said, a few women came to him privately expressing concern about JJ's "communication style and getting uptight under pressure." Conversations began to focus on changing the tactician, but there was no obvious replacement for

JJ on the team; a backup had not been trained. In a private dialogue, Leslie broached the possibility of replacing JJ with David.
Despite a great deal of effort, she and JJ were unable to establish a
peaceful equilibrium. "We kept asking ourselves, 'What can we
change?'" Leslie said. She knew from practicing together that she
worked well with David.

Vincent and Bill weighed Leslie's suggestion and discussed it
with some close advisers. When they called David in Connecticut
and asked him to consider coming aboard, he initially declined, but
he then accepted on condition that the team was in agreement.
One evening, when just a few days remained before the first semifinal race, Vincent and Bill called four women into Bill's office—
Leslie, Dawn, Stephanie Maxwell-Pierson, and Linda Lindquist.
"They were women whom we considered more influential," Bill
said, "women who see the big picture." The coaches were not
included in the meeting or much of the preliminary discussion
because, Bill said, "They wanted to keep things the way they were."

Sitting with their bosses in Bill's office, the four women were
asked to put aside their feelings for JJ. If they were assembling a
crew for a race, any race, next Saturday, which tactician would they
choose, JJ or David? The discussion was lengthy, and each woman
talked privately with Bill. In the end, they chose David.

The women's unanimous vote for David was heralded as a
"coming of age for women's sports," by some of the biggest names in
women's sports. The president of the Women's Sports Foundation,
Wendy Hilliard, and Anita DeFrantz, U.S. member of the elite
International Olympic Committee, publicly applauded the decision
to put David on board, saying it signaled our team's desire to win,
not just try. In the past, some women in male-dominated sports,

such as hockey and baseball, seemed more intent on piquing curiosity than pursuing victory. To some, our team was making an aggressive statement about our purpose on the race course.

The more common response to David's unceremonious appearance behind the wheel of *Mighty Mary* for the prestart of the first race of the semifinal was harsh criticism. *Did you push for this decision, or was it pushed on you?* The public and media wanted to know. Long after the fact, the question remains at issue.

A Management Move

Stephanie Maxwell-Pierson, one of the four women called into Bill's office, likened the decision to replace JJ to that of pulling a quarterback out of a losing game. She said: "They brought us in there to take the pulse of the team, not really to make a decision. They wanted to know what kind of reaction to expect. But I felt that even if we'd said, 'The women are going to hate this,' they still would have gone ahead with it."

Bill, on the other hand, said they would not have made the crew change if the four women had not supported it. He described the process in his office as "consensus-building." He said, "I kept asking, 'Do you want to win, or do you want to make a profound statement?' They all said they wanted to win. They were telling me this, but they didn't want to hurt JJ's feelings. I said, 'Look, I'll make the decision; I'll take the heat for it.'"

Bill may have intended to make a joint decision, but there was no precedent for team members—at the bottom of the America³ hierarchy—to make management decisions or crew selections. Leslie's involvement in the initial process of the decision makes it, to some extent, a team decision. But I'm not sure that it's correct to call the four women's vote, or the team's ultimate acceptance of the change, a "coming of age for women's sports." Instead, it seems more a reflection of the structure and daily functioning of America[3], which was based on the tacit understanding that David was a better tactician than JJ, Kimo a better driver than Leslie. Few of us had developed the confidence to rank ourselves above our more experienced coaches. It would have been nearly impossible for any of the women to say, "Yes, we want to win, *and* we think we have a better shot with JJ than David." Choosing to be winners implicitly meant choosing David.

DAVID DELLENBAUGH AND LESLIE

My sense that the team could have played only a small role in the decision to replace JJ with David was heightened one evening, a month after David joined our team. We were huddled around the TV screen, some people sitting on the floor, some sitting in folding chairs, many with bags of ice strapped to an aching body part. We were down to the wire, needing, somehow, to win all three of our remaining races to advance to the America's Cup. At the end of the video, Diana Klybert, one of the team's oldest and most outspoken members, jarred the group from our exhausted, disappointed daze. Diana stood at the back of our circle and suggested that we take a vote on whether we wanted to put JJ back on the boat for the next day's race. "Do we want to race what might be our last race tomorrow as an all-women's team?" she asked.

We were momentarily dumbstruck. JJ sat on the floor looking up at Diana. JJ had more or less accepted her demotion and had carved out a role helping to process weather data and develop strategy before races. She was as surprised as the rest of us that Diana had publicly broached the taboo subject of JJ's return to the race boat.

The ensuing conversation revealed that nearly everyone was shocked that Diana would ask us, the team, to make such an important decision. "There are so many factors involved in a decision that big—I just can't consider myself qualified to make such an important decision," said one of the four women who voted in Bill's office to replace JJ with David in the first place. "I don't feel like I've rotated onto the race boat enough times to have an informed opinion about what's best," someone said. "I haven't been a sailor long enough to really know," someone else said. One of the sailors sitting next to me suggested, "Maybe we should vote on whether we want to vote on this."

Ultimately, we took no vote. We simply asked Stu, the coach who was guiding us through the videos, to report our concerns to Vincent and Kimo.

I walked out of that meeting disappointed. David and JJ were two of my favorite people on the team, and voting would have been uncomfortable. But, I loved Diana's boldness. At that pivotal moment, I wanted to vote. I wanted our team to make a decision or, at the very least, to go down on record with an opinion.

But we had not been trained or encouraged to express divisive opinions or make independent decisions. From the very beginning of the campaign, the sailors' foremost concern was to be good team players. Big decisions were deferred to management. Our coaches consistently praised us for our superior attentiveness and cooperation. "They listen, they pay attention, they're more relaxed when you make suggestions," Kimo said of coaching women. "Guys have their own ideas about how to do everything; they don't change, they don't listen."

DAWN, JJ, AND STEPHANIE

As the bedrock of America[3], teamwork reaped enormous benefits for everyone. A capacity for cooperation and teamwork earned each of us a spot on the team and all the gifts that went with it—a rare chance to compete in the America's Cup and to learn the skills necessary to do so, the notoriety built into being a member of the historic, well-funded team, and all the presents in our mailboxes. By some sailors' accounts, an extraordinary commitment to teamwork made the women viable competitors against veterans the likes of Dennis Conner. Other sailors said that despite strong support from the public and the fifty other America[3] staff members, we never really became a team. I can't help but wonder if our virtue—our commitment to teamwork—wasn't also inherently linked to our biggest downfall. All that emphasis on cooperation and our sense that it would always be rewarded from above seemed to engender an element of passivity in our team.

As our short-lived revolutionary flame at the end of Round Two demonstrated, we never were able to coalesce into a strong, independently run team. We never stepped up to Bill, Vincent, or Kimo and demanded authority—demanded to skipper our own boat. Based on their experiences with men, our managers expected such a power struggle and took measures to avoid it. Oddly, they also seemed to be counting on us to fight for control. Bill and Vincent have repeatedly said they were puzzled when, early on, the women didn't come forward and insist on taking the reins of leadership. Instead of being crippled by the power struggles that had plagued the men in 1992, we seemed to settle into passing the buck. When difficult decisions needed to be made, we looked to our coaches, managers, and owner.

Bringing Aboard Confidence

At the time, discussions of the decision to put David on the boat focused on our team's inexperience. Looking back now, it's clear that our lack of autonomy and leadership were at the crux of the matter. More than anything, David brought confident leadership onto *Mighty Mary*.

Partly, David was able to lead by virtue of his experience. Leslie said that David did not come aboard and aggressively take over, but that he did bring with him a "quiet confidence" and a "wealth of knowledge." Dawn said much the same thing, "It was his confidence and experience that allowed us all to relax and focus on our own jobs." Moments of uncertainty were shored up by knowing that a proven well of competence stood in the back of the boat. Also, David's gentle demeanor blended well with Leslie's. Most important, David was the team's first *appointed* leader. For the first time, a crew member had more authority than our coaches—he had been installed over their heads. Off the boat, debriefings were notably different with David. For JJ, those evening reviews with the team and coaches in the sail loft seemed to be marked by high-pressure scrutiny of all her tactical decisions. We watched while JJ defended her thinking and strategy to the coaches. In contrast, David, who had been a coach before joining the crew, was rarely asked to justify his calls, win or lose.

David's unquestioned authority, along with his established rep-utation, contributed to the widely accepted perception that he came aboard and turned the team around. But in the final analysis, David and JJ had remarkably similar records on *Mighty Mary*. With seven wins, eleven losses, David won 39 percent of his races; with two wins, three losses, JJ won 40 percent of her races. Undoubtedly, David did bring expertise and peace to *Mighty Mary*. I can't help but think, though, of the lion who gets his badge of courage from the man behind the curtain and instantly becomes fearless, his roar deafening. Did some of what we sought from David and believed we received from him exist, unrecognized, inside of us?

Question of Leadership

"The hardest thing to do on a team is to put your personal feelings aside and bite your tongue or do what you wouldn't do for the good of the whole. The personal sacrifices and the rewards? They're there, but when you're caught up in it, they're hard to find sometimes."
—Annie Nelson's diary, March 23, 1995

"Total teamwork is idealistic; it is an educational theorem. It sounds great, but it doesn't necessarily work in real life."
—Dawn Riley

During one of the early rounds of racing, Bill had ridden along and observed from the seventeenth-man position in the back of the boat. A routine situation arose in which Leslie had too much pressure on the helm. She asked Merritt Palm, the starboard trimmer, to ease her jib sheet. Merritt eased, and seconds later Leslie asked for more ease. Again, Merritt eased. When

Leslie asked the third time, Merritt turned around and said, "I've already eased it a foot; how much more do you want?"

Bill said he watched in silent disbelief as "Merritt then called over [port-side trimmer Hannah Swett] and asked her if she thought the sail looked right. A ten-minute discussion followed. The point was that she did have the right sail shape, but Leslie had too much helm. Merritt couldn't have known that. She just had to trust Leslie's assessment, but she didn't because the crew did not have respect for anyone's leadership skills."

Bill was puzzled. Had a similar situation arisen among the men in '92, he said, helmsman Buddy Melges simply would have yelled, "EASE THE FUCKING SHEET, NOW." The incident would have been over in moments instead of wasting ten minutes. Bill asked the team sports psychologist for an explanation, and, "She told me that Merritt probably felt criticized by Leslie and went looking to Hannah for allegiance." He found the psychologist's reasoning believable, but odd, because men would never be offended by a similar request or lose focus on the task at hand to "worry about their feelings." Similarly, though, he said he once saw JJ and Leslie get so caught up in a disagreement that they sailed four hundred yards past the layline, the line on which the boat should tack to approach the mark.

A Void to Fill

In the first few rounds of racing, when we didn't win as many races as expected, Bill and Vincent crystallized our main problem as a lack of leadership. That's the void they were trying to fill, first when Vincent announced that Leslie was in charge on the race boat, and later when they put David aboard.

They believed the team was too wrapped up in our friendships and feelings to focus fully on winning or to let strong, dominant leadership emerge. "The women never did start coaching and criticizing each other on the boat. They couldn't get over the timidity of hurting each other's feelings," Vincent said. "It was hard for them to overcome that step of focusing on interpersonal relationships over everything else—like picking a leader."

JJ AND LESLIE

Vincent's perceptions of the men in 1992 were different. "They had developed a thick skin over a lifetime of being in a team situation—the mentality of leading and following came easily."

"I had to teach the men," Bill said, "to get along—to get them *not* to yell and criticize each other. My focus was teaching them to be less aggressive and assertive—to get their egos down below the ego of the boat." He said, though, that he couldn't "even bring the women's egos up to that of the boat."

Those team members who were aware of problems in the back of the boat saw a personality conflict between JJ and Leslie, not a lack of leadership. As a team, we *never* addressed the need to establish one clear position of authority on the boat. The rumor that management perceived a leadership problem entered our conversations, but the concept was treated as theoretical and remote from our real concerns. When David came aboard, and a "calm confidence" settled over the boat, most of us did not construe the improvement as leadership. We focused on his skills and experience and on the fact that his style meshed better with Leslie's.

In early August, Bill had consulted Anne Jardim, dean and co-founder of the Simmons Graduate School of Management, the country's only all-female business school, about the issue of leadership on our team. "I told Bill that I didn't think a leader would emerge," Jardim said, "that the women would have to be forced to come up with one. Women tend to generate teams of equals. We're not hierarchical—we operate by consensus. As a result, we don't generate leaders. Men are born followers. Women aren't. Men need to establish hierarchies, find leaders. Women don't." Shortly before racing began, Bill invited Jardim to hold a workshop with the team in San Diego, but the plans never came to fruition.

Jardim wasn't surprised that the team saw JJ and Leslie's struggle as a personality conflict instead of as a leadership void, or that we saw David's coming aboard as a better meshing of styles rather than as an infusion of leadership. "The very idea that groups need leadership has to be taught to women, and it should have been hammered into your group," Jardim said.

Is There a Difference?

Much psychological and sociological analysis of the differences between male and female behavior is based on the principle that, above all, women value interpersonal relationships and men value goals: career, creative, athletic. In her 1982, *In a Different Voice,* Carol Gilligan popularized the idea that where women see a web of relationships of which they want to be the center, men see a hierarchy they want to scale. Partially, the difference in value systems is traceable to the sexes' early play experiences. Boys learn the preeminence of rules and goals and the principles of leading and following by playing games built around them. Girls, on the other hand, engage in consensus-oriented "parallel play"—hopscotch and jump rope—where there are few rules. If someone is unhappy, it's easy simply to stop playing, and, if there is a winner, her success doesn't depend on her friend's failure.

In my years as a rower, I collected observations that seemed to support the idea that women value their friendships more than their athletic goals, and that we dislike establishing any sort of hierarchical order among ourselves. In college, the varsity crews were selected in the early spring through "seat racing." The coaches posted the afternoon's seat racing lineups in the window of a tobacco shop near campus. Those postings were little maps revealing who would face off later in the day. In turn, those races would establish in blunt terms who was the best, second-best, all the way down to the worst. We had trained year-round for a few precious months of competition. All the rowers, male and female, eagerly congregated to read our fate. I always envied the men their forthrightness. They could turn to each other and say something like, "I am gonna kick your ass this afternoon, but hey, you want to go get a beer afterward?" We women, on the other hand, with all the same time and effort invested and the same anticipatory adrenaline running through us, gave each other apologetic, worried looks and walked away in clouded tension.

Later, when I was coaching a high school girls' rowing team while training for the Olympic team, I was frustrated by the girls' requests not to seat race against each other. They were full of desire to prove themselves on the water, but they seemed to be saying that avoiding conflict with their friends was more important than fighting for a chance to be the best.

I've never really bought the popular theory that all of this can be traced to the playground, where boys play games with rules, winners and losers, and direct confrontation, while girls engage in games of house and tea parties. I, for one, grew up a vicious competitor, playing hopscotch *and* impishly dangling my swimming medals in front of my brother's envious eyes, abruptly folding up the Monopoly board when I thought I was losing. A passion for winning came just as naturally to me as being a loyal, compassionate friend. While the generation of women ahead of me and even women five years older might have grown up immersed in "parallel play," my generation and those following us have grown up on different playgrounds. In large part because of Title IX, the 1972 legislation mandating equal opportunities for girls in federally funded institutions, we've been raised with athletic competition. Many of us developed athletic identities beginning in primary school. Leslie and JJ grew up sailboat racers, and they learned to be winners before they were teenagers. And still, it appeared, they struggled to put aside their "personality conflict" for the sake of their common goal.

My athletic experience also leaves me suspicious of the theory that women truly *value* relationships more than goals. I've seen female athletes *focus* more on relationships than their male counterparts, but I've also seen them engage in psychological warfare that seems far more cruel than dumping ice water over someone in the bathroom. If women value feelings and relationships above their own aspirations, would they form exclusive cliques, gossip viciously behind each other's backs, politic against each other with coaches, and give each other the silent treatment—behavior I've witnessed among women at all levels of competition? To me, those methods are a distorted manifestation of the same well-developed competitive spirit and will to be the best that men are free to express overtly. Women just feel obligated to put a socially acceptable surface on their fire. Femininity, to which even the most competitive girls and women feel bound, does not include stringing your friends up the mast. Nor does it involve looking them in the eye and telling them you're going to kick their ass or, for that matter, telling them, "I'm in charge here, now EASE THE FUCKING SHEET."

Making Assumptions

The triage solution to *Mighty Mary's* "parallel play" problems was to inject leadership in the form of David Dellenbaugh. Bill said that if he could start again, he would design a management program that took into account the differences between men and women. "I firmly believe that women can be just as productive, efficient, and have the same killer instinct as men do," Koch said. "But getting to that point takes a different technique. If they are focused on relationships, then let's use that to our advantage and work on areas where they are weak. For men, those techniques have been worked out over centuries in wars and on the playing fields."

Female athletes, conditioned to be as nice and polite as they are ambitious, may require a different coaching/management system than male athletes, as Bill suggests. But the prescription may not call for taking advantage of women's being "focused on relationships."

"When making assumptions about how to manage women," said Deborah Kolb, an expert in gender issues, organizational structures, negotiation and conflict resolution, who is a professor at Simmons College and a senior fellow in the Program on Negotiation at Harvard Law School, "people frequently assume that women will do better when the focus is on consensus, not one clear voice of authority." She said eliminating the skipper position from our team was a good example of this tendency. But that divorces what is actually happening from the task. "On your boat, you had a lot of split-second decisions to make. Like managing any crisis, you needed one person in charge, not a lot of people discussing and disagreeing. When setting up these systems, the question should be, 'What is the best structure for the situation?' regardless of gender. It almost never is."

In trying to build strong teams and bring out the best in girls and women in competitive situations, it doesn't make sense to tell them,

"You're girls, so you know how to get along and be good team players."
Instead, they should be organized in systems that fit the tasks at hand,
as Kolb suggests, and then taught something they may never have
learned before—to embrace the competitive beast inside. Female
athletes should not necessarily emulate males, but direct confrontation and the clear expression of competitive passion to be the best
should be encouraged. We should not be held to special standards of
"feminine" cooperativeness, attentivenesss, or niceness. Unfettered
competition doesn't take anything away from being compassionate,
commanding, or collaborative, all of which women are.

Pat Summitt, head coach of the University of Tennessee's four-
time NCAA national champion women's basketball team, said
teamwork has been a fundamental theme throughout her twenty-
two years of coaching. But Summitt's interpretation of teamwork is
different from the way the principle was applied at America^3, and
from the way it is often applied to women's teams. Summitt played
to an Olympic silver medal in 1976, and coached the U.S. women to
their first gold in 1984. She believes teamwork means "giving everyone a key role to play and then telling them to lead, follow, or get
out of the way." Summitt added that building and maintaining
strong teams "is not about keeping a smooth surface on things. It's
crucial to teach women to be honest and confrontational with each
other—to face conflict head-on."

Kolb reinforces Summitt's point about conflict and teams. She
said that she sees conflict as a "perennial feature of organizations"
and that "women are socialized to keep conflict quiet, to see conflict as a threat." But Kolb sees a role for conflict in fostering cooperation and high performance. "There's a sense that somehow good

teamwork has no conflict, but the way to get good teams is to surface and resolve conflict," Kolb said.

Confrontation and conflict resolution were not included in the
America[3] coaching system. Repeated disagreements and struggles
for power among the men's team in 1992 led Bill, Vincent, and Kimo
to emphasize cooperation and positive attitudes with the women
three years later. They did not foresee that as women, our team
might need extra lessons in productively handling tense interpersonal situations and disagreements. In fact, there seemed to be the
perception that because we were women, conflict should be kept to
a minimum. When Bill asked Kimo why two of our most talented
and accomplished guest coaches—Buddy Melges and John
Kolius—always coached the B-boat instead of the A-boat when
they came to town, Bill said, "Kimo told me those guys were too
loud and critical and that they upset the women for days afterward." Expertise was traded for tranquility. Even Dick Dent said he
modified his coaching style to fit what he saw as the women's intol-
erance of confrontation. When he yelled things like, "What's the
matter, are you a wimp, you can't even do fifteen push-ups?" at the
men's team in '92, he got results. From the women, he got tears. He
decided to rely on polite explanations instead of direct challenges
with the women.

We were not conditioned to handle confrontation with our
coaches or among ourselves. The premium was on harmony.
Tolerating and avoiding disputes and sticky issues was the most
acceptable way of handling conflict. When conflict arose, as it
inevitably did, particularly between JJ and Leslie, our team, from
top to bottom, was ill-equipped to deal with it overtly.

Despite our team-player training, the women of America[3] did at times yell at one another about crossed lines and botched maneuvers. Brief, to-the-point communication—along with heated emotions—is built into the sport. A boat doesn't make it around a mark without some of each.

Unresolved Confrontations

As Bill Koch witnessed, other confrontations—especially those between the two people with the most responsibility, JJ and Leslie—were protracted, sometimes becoming personal, destructive forces. Those unresolved confrontations seemed to get in the way of strong, unencumbered leadership. However, I don't believe we had leadership problems because the women of America[3] cared less about winning than they did about their relationships, as some theorized later. Nor do I believe it's because we grew up having tea parties, since nearly all of us had been competitors from an early age. I saw predatory instincts in all the women, as well as hard-nosed, thick-skinned, I'm-telling-you-how-it-is leadership capabilities in most members of the afterguard, particularly JJ and Dawn. Those two women proved their leadership skills when they got *Mighty Mary* safely and victoriously around the course on a challenging day of racing that sent *oneAustralia* to the bottom of the ocean and Dennis Conner back to the dock.

Given the abilities of JJ and Dawn, it seems legitimate to ask why as a group we never fully coalesced around them. Why didn't we recognize the need to have strong leadership and then hand that role to one or two of our teammates?

DAVID DELLENBAUGH

America[3]'s leadership void fits the patterns Anne Jardim has consistently found in twenty years of research. Women are "unwilling to follow" and have difficulty organizing themselves hierarchically. Coach Pat Summitt has a somewhat different view. She said that "not all great leaders are born," but that she does see natural leaders and natural followers among the women who come through her basketball program. When she described the natural leaders, she seemed to be describing at least a few of the women on our team: "Leaders are those who see the big picture, who have opinions, who are comfortable speaking up in a group. Leaders aren't easily intimidated; they're not afraid of the moment or of being different." Unlike those who ran the America[3] program, Summitt said, she constantly strives to develop leadership among her team members. "It's something we work on and talk about *all the time.*"

Dawn Riley, who has a wealth of experience sailing with male and female crews, has her own theory about women and leadership. "Women might not respect other women as much, so they are not willing to be led by them. When you win a women's regatta, you think, 'Oh, I only beat the women's league.' Men think and know they are the best. And so there is no question or doubt in their minds about their leaders. They can think, 'As long as he's good, I'll follow him.'" As Jardim put it, "Women superimpose their doubts about themselves onto their potential leaders."

Dawn's theory rings true for our group. Perhaps David's gentle command was so easily accepted when he came aboard simply because he is a man. Realistically, accepting leadership from among our own would have required at least a small leap of faith. Buddy Melges's maturity and unparalleled sailing accomplishments garnered him respect at the wheel that no one on our team could have matched. In part, our team was simply too young. But, even a woman Buddy's age could not have chalked up a comparable list of successes—the opportunities have not been available.

As much as our weak internal leadership stemmed from the fact that we are women, it was rooted in the way the management system was implemented. Although management's intention was to take the successful 1992 system and simply insert women, our program ended up being quite different than the men's. It bore similarities, though, to the way in which women have been fit into organizational structures for decades. Despite the best intentions to break down barriers and empower women, even within America[3], our junior status was institutionalized.

A diagram of the America[3] power structure would put us at the bottom of four tiers. The team fell beneath Kimo, who was on a level with the other program directors. The only woman on the middle-management level was Linda Lindquist, co-director of marketing. As a sailing team member, she was in the odd position of also falling under Kimo. Vincent was up on the next rung. Only Bill topped him.

In 1992, many people filled the same roles, but the structure of the organization was significantly different. In '92, the coaches (a different staff) had no real authority; they were advisers, not leaders. The leaders were members of the sailing team. People jumped at helmsman Buddy Melges's command partly because he had Bill, the skipper, the owner, the embodiment of authority, standing beside him, backing him.

Our team, on the other hand, didn't always jump when JJ, Dawn, or Leslie spoke because the real voices of authority—Bill, Vincent, and Kimo—were not sailing on the boat. When JJ and Leslie struggled to make this situation work under conditions that called for unquestioned leadership, their difficulties were widely viewed as a clash of personalities instead of a problem with the system.

The team's subordinate position in the hierarchy meant that our own leaders' authority was easily overridden or undermined from above. Dawn said her simple requests—such as installing a phone in the boat pens or waiting to scrub the boat's waterline until the morning—were often put off or denied. "I almost started getting a persecution complex," Dawn said. "Sometimes I felt like screaming, 'We're trying to win an America's Cup campaign here; can anybody help us?' I always felt like I was stepping on somebody's toes when I expressed my opinion. The people who were in control, who just happened to be men, were not sharing it with the people who were not in control."

Dawn and Annie Nelson, two of the most experienced sailors among us, said they routinely felt their expertise dismissed by coaches. Dawn describes it as "responsibility without authority."

For example, she said, "I said in meetings all the time, 'We need to know what the designers are trying to accomplish so that we can incorporate it into the way we sail.' But the coaches and Vincent never listened. We had no input. When I asked Kimo directly about design questions, he told me, 'You don't need to know that.' I was shut off. There was an attitude from above of, 'You little girls run along. We'll take care of it.'" Annie, who has been sailing for more than twenty years, said that one time when she expressed her concern about some new sails, "one of the coaches actually told me not to worry my pretty little head about it."

A Young Influence

Our junior status was exacerbated because the women started the campaign knowing much less than the coaches. Our deficit of America's Cup experience made us attentive, but also, unfortunately, it made it harder for us to be confident in ourselves and in one another.

Kimo's natural good rapport with some of the youngest women on the team, the "Fab Four," contributed to our sense of subordination. We saw that those young, talented sailors looked up to Kimo as a big brother. He had breakfast and went mountain biking with them on rare days off, and he consulted them about crew selections and other decisions. Their protected status on and off the race boat set up a strange *Lord of the Flies* dynamic, in which some of the least mature people tacitly wielded power and influence within the team.

Kimo said after the campaign: "There was never a decision made without consulting the women first. We didn't push anything on them." But we did not *make* the decisions. The avenues of authority open to the women were what Deborah Kolb described as "classic low-power techniques:" Currying favor with the real power figures, counting on friendships, building allegiances, and petty politics.

A Backroom Deal

When *Mighty Mary* left the dock the morning of the last race of the semifinals competition, our team faced two extreme possibilities. PACT '95 had already earned its berth in the finals, and the last race was sudden death between us and Dennis. If we won, we would go down in the record books as the women's team that eliminated Dennis Conner, the biggest name in America's Cup competition. No matter what happened afterward, that feat alone would be a mark of distinction, proof of our worthiness. Losing would relegate us to last place. The reason for our endless hours of practice and multimillion-dollar budget—and maybe even the future of women in the Cup—would be thrown into question.

"It felt like we had twice as much pressure going into that race as we ever had before," Dawn said. "We knew everyone was standing by to judge us. We couldn't afford one mistake."

People were watching that race all over the country. ESPN elected to televise the event after initially planning to begin broadcasting with the finals. Public interest had been stirred by a bitter off-the-water battle between our syndicate and Team Dennis Conner. Dennis replaced a faulty keel—one he claimed nearly fell off in a race—with an older one. The different keel, and other modifications the *Stars and Stripes* team made to accommodate it, appeared to make the boat faster in light wind conditions. Equipment changes in the middle of a round of racing are strictly regulated, and we thought Dennis should be disqualified. While the racing continued, we protested to the International Jury, the body charged with enforcing the Citizen's Cup rules. When the Defense Committee members heard of our protest, they instructed the jury not to hear it. Three of the five men on the committee were ex-commodores of the San Diego Yacht Club, and so was Dennis. We were behind the eight ball. When America[3] threatened a lawsuit, the Defense Committee finally relinquished the protest decision to the International Jury. They found Dennis's keel change illegal. The jury threw out the race he'd won against us after the switch and ordered a resail.

Time for a Payback

By chance, the resail became the deciding race for both teams. Win or go home. For our team, the race was also a chance to settle a score with Dennis. In our estimation, he had cheated, and yet there he was, still with a chance to advance. More than athletic interests were at stake. Making it into the finals was crucial business for the syndicates because the beginning of regular television coverage meant important sponsor payback.

"We didn't talk much on the tow out," Dawn said, describing the mood aboard *Mighty Mary* as the crew headed for the starting line for the last do-or-die race. "Everyone was trying to stay calm." The light and shifting wind conditions favored Dennis, but David Dellenbaugh nudged ahead of *Stars and Stripes* off the start, beginning what was nearly a perfect race for *Mighty Mary*. On the final leg, *Stars and Stripes* was a quarter mile—nearly six minutes— behind. Sly smiles started to creep onto the faces of our crew. As Leslie brought the bow of *Mighty Mary* over the finish line and the gun fired, signaling the women's victory, the team rejoiced, cheering, clapping, and hugging one another. The unsinkable was sunk. The first all-women's team in America's Cup history had cleared the biggest hurdle yet. No one could say we didn't belong.

CELEBRATION—SHORT-LIVED

"That moment," said Stephanie Maxwell-Pierson, "was the happiest of the campaign. We proved that we could sail under incredible pressure and beat Dennis at his own game."

Moments later, Vincent, Kimo, and Bill jumped aboard. Their solemn faces puzzled the crew. As the onboard ESPN cameras rolled, the men told the team that the race hadn't mattered. A backroom deal had been cut. Regardless of the outcome of the race, all three boats would advance to the Citizen's Cup finals. Dennis was still in. When push came to shove, Dennis and Bill had gotten cold feet. Neither wanted to risk his whole campaign on the outcome of a single race. PACT, already qualified for the next round, signed off on the deal after securing favorable seeding in the finals. The women on *Mighty Mary* couldn't believe it and tried to hide their disappointment from the cameras. "I was really pissed," Dawn said. "We sailed a great race, and then it meant nothing."

Many sailors described finding out about the deal as "the worst moment of the campaign." Stephanie said, "It was so disappointing and frustrating to have our accomplishment taken away from us."

That afternoon was not the first time our team had heard of the three-boat final. One evening about a week before, shortly after the keel protests and vitriol began, Bill assembled the team in the sail loft. Should we continue protesting and pursuing a lawsuit, he asked, or did we want to accept a compromise allowing all three teams into the finals? The idea had been broached at the negotiating table as a possible solution to the dispute over Dennis's keel change.

No one had ever heard of a three-way final in the America's Cup. The concept broke new ground even in a game whose history is rich with last-minute rules revisions and executive privilege.

The first time the New York Yacht Club sponsored the race in 1870, it fielded fourteen yachts against Britain's single yacht in a race widely regarded as unfair. The following year, after agreeing to field only one defender against Britain's one challenger, the New York Yacht Club reserved the right to choose its "one" defender day-to-day from among four yachts. It took years for the ill winds to die down.

A hundred years later, a new tempest was brewing. We wanted Dennis disqualified. We voted against the deal and assumed that was the last we'd hear of it.

The night before our sudden death face-off against Dennis, Bill gathered us to take another vote. He announced that the three-boat final was still a possibility because of ongoing protests related to the keel change. We had lost badly to Dennis that day, and given the weather forecast, our chances on the race course did not look good for the next day. We voted to accept the three-boat final if it could be brokered.

The three syndicates negotiated late into the night, but could not come up with a plan that had incentives for everyone. When *Mighty Mary* left the dock for the final race against Team Dennis Conner, the deal had not been made. We would have to prove ourselves on the water to eliminate Dennis and get into the finals.

Dennis started the race knowing it was not the do-or-die situation that our team believed it was. PACT had phoned America[3] at 4:00 A.M. the day of the race to start negotiating yet again, and a deal was made one hour before our race. Dennis's team was told about the last-minute turn of events, but our team wasn't. As Vincent explained, "We wanted them to go through a do-or-die situation with all that pressure on them."

Angry Storm Rising

When the story broke, poison pens flew. *Sports Illustrated* was incredulous: "By changing the rules as it sails along, the America's Cup has lost its place on the sports map." The writer called the America's Cup TEGWAR—The Exciting Game Without Any Rules and said the game had more in common with politics than sports.

It wasn't just the media. The deal and the shenanigans behind it angered many fans as well. Owners in other sports were not permitted to get together and change the rules in the middle of a game. Why should anyone, people asked, take the event seriously when what happened at the negotiating table mattered more than what happened on the water?

Looking back, Bill sees the deal as a mistake, "We set out to enhance the credibility of the America's Cup in the public's eye, and we put a ding in it instead." Perhaps even worse, Bill sees the decision to accept the deal as a measurement of how much—or how little—the America³ management and sailors believed in our team's ability. "It was a vote of no confidence by us and the team," he said. "We sure as hell would not have made that choice in '92."

The workings of the deal seemed consistent with my sense that our team, at times, was overpowered by the big guys, the real players, in the America's Cup game. We played a role in the decision by voting for it. But the next morning, our role was undermined when we were sent to the starting line believing we were racing for our lives.

Even though the deal tarnished the credibility of the America's Cup and momentarily cast our team as pawns on the public stage, I was struck by how little it seemed to matter to most fans of the women's team. The machinations behind the deal were so complicated that many people were left confused and simply chose to blame Dennis for weaseling his way into the finals. But the deal, and America³'s involvement in it, seemed irrelevant to most of our fans. It may be true, as *Sports Illustrated* asserted, that the America's Cup had "lost its place on the sports map," but from the very beginning, our team had spilled off the sports map. Like that of Olympic heroes, our team's appeal transcended the country's corps of sports fans and armchair athletes. We attracted a broad following of patriots whose support seemed nearly unconditional.

The extraordinary meaning of our team was never more clear to me than the day our compound hosted a breast cancer fundraiser around the time the three-boat deal started to brew. Candace Anderson, who was married to our head sailmaker, Per, and who suffered from breast cancer, organized "Sail for a Cure." We gave boatloads of visitors hundred-dollar rides aboard *America³* The passengers either held on and watched in overwhelmed silence, or they participated by taking a turn on the grinding handles or at the helm. Diana Klybert and Annie Nelson, performers at heart, rose to the occasion, giving enthusiastic introductions to safety aboard our "fine yacht" *America³* and her "hearty crew members."

On one ride, a woman well over sixty came aboard on the arm of her husband. She stood, pale, jaw clamped tight, at the front edge of the cockpit and gripped the hip-level rail behind her. She appeared so uncomfortable pitching with every motion of the boat and looking worriedly for the sources of all its creaks and groans that I considered asking her if she wanted us to call the tender to take her to shore. Instead, I tried to make small talk. Yes, she nodded her gray head, she had been following the women's team from the beginning. No, she hadn't cared much about sailing until she'd heard of us. That was all she had to say until the end of the half-hour when we came to a stop, bow into the wind. Finally, she smiled. "I've never had a diary before," she said quietly. "I think I'm going to start a diary today. Being on this boat with all you women was the most important day of my life, and I want to write it down."

Showdown Time

In our first race against Dennis in the three-way final, the regular spinnaker halyard broke, and the spare flew out of control and out of our reach to the top of the mast. We had no chance of cutting into Dennis's lead unless we could somehow get hold of the spare halyard to fly a spinnaker on the last downwind leg. The other halyards on the boat go only three-quarters of the way up the mast. We could hoist someone to that point, and then she would have to free-climb the last thirty feet while the boat pounded its way upwind. It was a task not unlike trying to shinny up a flagpole during an earthquake. Merritt Carey and Lisa Charles each volunteered. "My first reaction was 'No, it's too dangerous,'" David Dellenbaugh said later, "but then I realized that if they were men, I would let them try. So, I did." Merritt and Lisa were unsuccessful, but some of the women holding their breath watching from the deck below described the effort as the most heroic moment of the campaign.

In another battle against Dennis, *Mighty Mary* had the lead. As Leslie brought the boat around the last mark, *Stars and Stripes*, approaching the mark from the other direction, veered head-on into *Mighty Mary's* path. Leslie was forced to push out of the way, sharply into the wind. The newly hoisted spinnaker filled with so much pressure that the pole snapped. The last several feet of the carbon fiber, cannon like pole crashed down on Susie Nairn's head. Susie suffered a mild concussion, but she managed not to be thrown from her position on the narrow, slippery, lurching bow. The team hustled to bring the spare spinnaker pole up from below and secure it in place. *Mighty Mary* maintained her lead to the finish.

Twice the score was tied during the course of the finals—perhaps the best indication of the women's viability as America's Cup sailors. Dennis lost only a few races, and toward the end of the twelve-race series, he fought his way into the lead. PACT, on the other hand, settled into a losing streak that became a dramatic reversal of fortune for what had been the favored boat.

Collaboration between America³ and PACT before one of the last races irked Dennis Conner. Usually, opposing camps maintain a Cold War air. Boats pass each other on the water without acknowledgment. News conferences are frigidly polite. But PACT had to win the next race against Dennis in order for both of our teams to stay in the fight. We had a stake in their winning, and putting aside hostilities came naturally because Annie Nelson's husband, Bruce, worked for PACT as chief designer and strategist.

An Intimate Exchange

Diana Klybert sent over a pair of her underwear, a good luck charm to be flown from PACT's rig during the race. Soon, we got a delivery of PACT '95 insignia light blue boxer shorts, a pair for everyone on the team. The PR department received several unhappy phone calls from people who felt let down by such raunchy, juvenile behavior by their heroines. Sandra Bateman, associate director of communications and public relations, patiently defended the underwear exchange as a small release from the mounting pressure.

Dennis's camp objected to the fact that we kicked in our superior weather data gathering capabilities to PACT's benefit. Perhaps more objectionable was that *Mighty Mary* gave PACT's *Young America* an on-the-water warm-up for the race, a big help to a program operating with only one boat. Dennis told the local paper that we were ganging up on him.

PACT trounced Dennis, giving us our second major showdown against Dennis. If we won, Dennis was out, and only one final race remained between us and PACT. If Dennis won, he would go on to defend the America's Cup.

LAST RACE

During that crucial race between us and Dennis, my mother said, she sat glued to her television set. She was one of many people whom the women's team turned into fans of the America's Cup. Over the course of the two-week Citizen's Cup finals, my mother and her friend Glenda Mardock did not miss a second of coverage from their post in Glenda's Kansas City living room. In Seoul and

Barcelona, my mother enjoyed the sights and food more than the Olympic events. But she could rattle off the women's names and, to my disbelieving ears, Dennis Conner's stats. I wasn't on the race boat during the finals, but she knew I was behind the scenes. She, like many other women of her generation, were drawn to the team because so many people said we couldn't do it. After sixty years of living, she had a different idea about women's capabilities. She scheduled her chemotherapy appointments around the races. Even through her Danish accent, she perfected a mincing, nasal imitation of Dennis. His arrogance and condescending attitude toward the women's team, she said, "made me grow a terrible dislike for the man." By the time the final race against Dennis rolled around, she and Glenda, seeing Dennis's face on the screen, either turned off the TV or held pillows up to their faces to block the view.

On the day of our final sail-off against Dennis, my mother and Glenda watched and chatted about the women's fine sailing. Without warning, baseball appeared on the screen. *Mighty Mary* had gotten a small lead at the start, which the crew extended to more than four minutes at the final turning mark. The lazy wind had died, half-knot by half-knot, throughout the race. ESPN, which was stuck with showing boats that were barely moving as well as the huge margin between the boats, cut away.

Mother and Glenda were not as confident as ESPN that the women had the race wrapped up when they watched *Mighty Mary* come around the last mark and head over to the right side of the course. "We had been watching Conner's crew, and they were not giving up," my mother said later. "I had a terrible feeling that he would slither over to that center line and get ahead of the women." They went to bed wondering if the women had finally pulled the plug on Dennis. Most people I have talked to since said they shut off their televisions certain that the women's team had won. They were shocked by the results in their newspapers the next day.

The corks were still in the champagne aboard *Chubasco* and back at the compound during the final legs of the race, but more and more bottles were put on ice in anticipation of the biggest celebration yet.

As I watched from the sidelines, my biggest concern was that the wind would fade so badly that *Mighty Mary* would be unable to complete the race in the requisite four hours. Christy Evans and I had been dispatched in a small motor boat that morning to a point one mile above the weather mark to radio wind speed and direction to Dawn Riley aboard *Mighty Mary* for several hours before the start. The meager readings we'd gotten that morning had built slightly and then begun to die through the course of the day. In such light wind, the first five legs of the race were uneventful. We had a confident upper hand over Dennis, and it looked like only a miracle could save him. As *Mighty Mary* came around the last mark, Christy and I followed her so we could be at the finish line to cheer our team's victory.

We motored over to the right side of the course. A boatload of PACT supporters puttered along next to us. When radio announcer Bob Fisher said that *Stars and Stripes* had come around the windward mark a full four minutes behind *Mighty Mary*, we looked over at the people who would be our foes the next day, and all of us let out a simultaneous cheer.

Playing a Shift

Christy glanced back with a furrowed brow. "Dennis seemed to come around in more breeze," she said. A native of Marblehead, Massachusetts, Christy had been racing sailboats most of her life. Often, she could predict the next turn of events. But this time I had to laugh at her, "Come on, Christy," I said, "*we're half a mile ahead.* Relax. They're not going to catch us."

When *Mighty Mary* came around the mark, David Dellenbaugh knew he couldn't take victory for granted, and he had a tough call to make. Classic match racing strategy calls for covering, or staying between your opponent and the finish line. But with such a huge lead, covering would have required two jibes. Jibing in very light wind costs time, and it's risky because the deflated spinnaker can easily get caught on the rig and rip as it's pulled to the other side of the boat. David chose to round the mark and keep his course to the favored right-hand side, where the breeze and current were usually better in the afternoon.

MIGHTY MARY

Dennis came around the mark, and, with his whole campaign apparently finished, he took a gamble. Within thirty seconds of rounding, he jibed to the left, and he found what he was hoping for—better breeze. David called for a jibe in an effort to cover. But, with better wind on Dennis's side of the course, *Stars and Stripes* ate up—in less than half the time—the same distance toward the finish line that *Mighty Mary* had covered in four minutes.

We watched as the two boats engaged in a slow motion jibing duel. *Mighty Mary's* jibes looked labored. Over the radio, Fisher, who was allowed a closer vantage point than we, explained that the crew was having a hard time getting the main sail battens—the rods that stiffen the upper part of the sail—to flip through in the jibes. The inside-out main was slowing *Mighty Mary*. The next time the boats zigzagged together, Dennis was practically on top of us. We found out later that he had closed our forty-two boat length lead to less than two.

Fisher called it the most dramatic comeback in the history of the America's Cup. Standing next to me in the tender, Christy could not hold back her frustration. I could not believe my eyes. I knew about sprinting from behind, but this was ridiculous. The next time the boats crossed, Dennis had rolled over the top of us.

For a moment, I wasn't sure why Christy had let out a shriek of joy. In a jibe that seemed within an arm's reach of our tender, *Stars and Stripes* blew out their spinnaker. *Mighty Mary* now had one more chance to win. Christy and I looked at each other, "OK, that's it, here we come, they're out," we coaxed.

Finding a good puff of wind as *Stars and Stripes* struggled with its spinnaker, *Mighty Mary* came within a half-boat length of regaining the lead. But in less than a minute, *Stars and Stripes*— loaded with sailors who had recovered from hundreds of shredded spinnakers in their days—was flying a new spinnaker and inching toward the finish line, still in the lead.

Dennis's team finished two boat lengths—or fifty-two seconds in the dead wind—ahead of the women. As soon as their navy blue bow crossed the line and the gun fired designating them the winners and the official defenders, those men did, as Bill Koch said, jump up and down, slap each other on the back, and holler like they had just won the World Series. They had.

Their celebration was an unintended tribute to the capability and fighting spirit of the women's team, but it was hard to watch. The entire America[3] team—the sailors aboard *Mighty Mary* and all the rest of us spread around the course on boats or writing news releases or answering phones back at the compound—was still recovering from the horror of watching a lead secured during three hours dissolve in a matter of moments. The sailors focused on the mechanics of dropping the spinnaker and getting down the main sail. Wordless hugs were exchanged. The team busied themselves derigging the boat and packing up gear.

DENNIS CONNER'S CREW IS JUBILANT

Some tears flowed, some were stifled. "I thought I was going to break into a million pieces when we lost," Katie Pettibone said later. Katie was twenty-two years old, the second-youngest member of the team. As a starboard trimmer, she held one of the high pressure spots, and she's anything but fragile. "To have lost like that—well, the grief was enormous," Katie said. "Going back to the dock, I didn't know what to expect. I felt like we had let so many down. So we get there, and the dock is *full* of everyone in the compound to cheer us and support us. It was a fantastic thing. We lost, but we lost together, and we would have won together."

Even before *Mighty Mary* had reached the dock late that afternoon, the America³ fax machines were on fire. "What the women's team has done for sailing and sports, women and aspiration, and the meaning of team spirit and sportsmanship is what the history books are recording," wrote a woman in one of the first faxes to reach the compound. Good wishes came from all over the country and as far away as Switzerland and New Zealand. Sponsors and senators sent their congratulations. We received many simple, "We love you's."

Being Competitive

I have read over my copies of that pile of faxes dozens of times. To me, as much as any other official recognition given the women's team, they are a measurement of what we accomplished. The women's team fell short of winning, but even so, we achieved much more than most people predicted. When we started the campaign, few believed we could match the physical strength of the men's team, but once the racing began, the strength issue was never raised again. When our team was announced, the prevailing view was that we would do little more than get the boat around the course, but we proved to pose a serious competitive threat.

Many of the faxes that came into the compound after the race read like testimonials to these achievements: "Having a women's team to cheer for made us feel like we had a right to be watching. You have taught millions of women about sailing, competition, and winning. We have learned it's OK to be physical, and we can do anything if we set our minds to it. You have altered the way we think about ourselves forever. We believe that it is well worth the personal and financial price you had to pay. But, then again, how do you put a price on the self-esteem of millions of women?" wrote a group of seven women and one man who gave only their first names and did not say where they were from.

The women's team seemed to transcend the harsh line between winners and losers normally drawn by sports fans. Getting across the finish line in anything but first place is usually cause for fan desertion. Despite the results, though, the courage and capability of our team was celebrated across the country for months afterward.

Athletes are usually their own harshest judges. David Dellenbaugh was proof. Several days after the last race, Bill said, he found David packing up his things in the compound, and David was still upset and tearful over the final race. But the team recognized our triumphs despite our final loss. Not long after the campaign, the women talked about having proved that we could "compete at the highest level of sailing," that if "we could sail IACC yachts, we could sail anything," that we had "opened doors," "inspired people to dream bigger than ever," and "changed the history of the sport."

After a year of mastering the routine of doing what we weren't supposed to be able to do, each woman left America^3 with a greater sense of her own possibilities. At a party at Bill's house the night after the race, most of us were already planning our next challenges, many of which would be bigger and heartier for the new opportunities opened by our campaign. Some looked toward the America's Cup in 2000, some started planning Olympic campaigns for 1996, or the next Whitbread, or breaking into the world match-racing circuit. Several women anticipated converting their America^3 experience into opportunities outside of sailing—business, PhDs in sports psychology, or women's psychology.

Despite the confidence many of us gained by being a part of the team, to some within the world of yachting we appeared to be, as I sensed at the yacht club the evening after our last race, more of a nuisance than evidence of women's capability. Shortly after the cup, Kimo raced to Hawaii on a boat with some men from PACT and Dennis's team. "There was some respect, but more jokes," Kimo said, wincing as he remembered them. "They hated the women; not personally, but they didn't think the women would win one race, and they hated the fact that they'd done so well—maybe the women's team just opened the door a little bit. But most of my friends whom I sail with all the time don't have any time for women. I'd sail with them anytime, though."

Learning From Rosie

I couldn't help but see Rosie the Riveter, a constant presence through our campaign, as a warning sign predicting a hostile reaction to our team from some corners. Rosie graced the front of our team T-shirt, one of America³'s most popular retail items. Her wartime productivity slogan, "We Can Do It," runs as a balloon in bold letters across the top of her picture. Initially, I loved those shirts. The message connected our team to a long line of women who have heroically worked and struggled. Rosie looks tough rolling up her sleeves, clenching her fist, and showing some biceps. Her head is cocked back, and her blue eyes gaze out directly from the shirt. Her face has a pugnacious expression just short of a scowl. But as much as Rosie provided inspiration, she also told a story of disappointment. By doing men's work, Rosie posed a threat to the standards of femininity and the balance of power between the sexes. A closer look at her reveals her carefully plucked and shaped eyebrows, her inhumanly long eyelashes, and her badge of domesticity, the red kerchief with white polka dots.

Rosie is an emblem of women's strength, *and* she is a symbol of our limitations in a system controlled by men. Rosie filled in; she did not revolutionize. When the soldiers came home, they went back to work. Rosie returned to her homebound periphery.

Bill Koch believes our team carved out a brighter immediate future for women in sailing than Rosie did for women in the work force. "Women *can* do it; that's the real lesson here," Bill said. "The fact that so many of the old guard despised the women and wished they would just fade away is an indication of how really powerful the women's team was. Now we know that the formula for winning is different for women. The team did well, but if we'd taught them leadership and how to handle conflict and confrontation, they could have gone even further."

Bill is among many fans who saw our team as true pioneers— win or lose, we successfully navigated through uncharted territory and cleared a path for those behind us. A post-race fax that seems to say just that is the one that means the most to me. It came from a family in San Francisco:

"Hold up your heads, you are heroes to us and our baby daughter, Marty. A lot of good teams will not be in the America's Cup, but none accomplished so much in so little time. You have made history and changed the world a bit for the better for little girls like Marty. She'll remember and honor the '95 America[3] campaign when she sails for the America's Cup twenty years from now."

Women's names may not crowd the rosters of the next America's Cup teams, or even the ones after that. But another generation of girls will *not* grow up watching and thinking to themselves, "I'm a girl. I can't do that."

Afterword

Six months after our around-the-clock campaign for the America's Cup came to an abrupt end, I mailed questionnaires across the country and a few across the oceans to my twenty-eight teammates. Among other things, I asked people to describe a heroic moment that stood out in their minds. Not everyone responded, but of the majority who did, several said Merritt Carey and Lisa Charles displayed heroism in their efforts to free-climb the mast and retrieve the spinnaker halyard. JJ Isler's name came up most frequently: "JJ was instrumental in the development of the team." "Stepping down as tactician to let a man take over, I think of all the sacrifices that were made throughout the year, this had to be the toughest to handle." "She showed a ton of courage." One person said David Dellenbaugh was heroic "for accepting the position and having to go to that first press conference." A few people said the B-boat crew had been heroes; some people said our whole team had been heroes "for the transformation from not believing in itself to magical racing."

Others named the shore crew the heroes for their "incredible patience" and "incredible hours." Someone thought Dennis Conner's team had shown the most heroism in their comeback during the last race against *Mighty Mary*, which "proved that nothing is impossible if you stick together, work hard, and have a little luck to capitalize on." A couple of people said there were no heroes: "Heroic is a strong word."

All ten questions, including queries about people's backgrounds, what the team accomplished, and the definition of teamwork, elicited a dramatic array of answers. We had had widely different experiences going into the campaign, and we each had our own experience *of* the campaign. The story told here is uniquely mine.

"Will there be another women's team?" Nearly a year after we sailed our last race, that's the question that comes up most often when I talk about my America's Cup experience. People seem to view our team as an enormous success, and they want to see our effort as a precious legacy. Many seem disappointed to hear that the women of America³ quickly fanned out to jobs, school, speaking tours, Olympic campaigns, or other sailing adventures—*we should be getting ready for Auckland in 2000*. We knew from the start that Bill Koch would not be backing another women's team, but several women from our team, led by Dawn Riley, have announced The San Francisco Challenge, a men's and women's campaign for 2000 of which Dawn is CEO. The future of women in the America's Cup is now up to a fabulously wealthy and generous individual, or group of corporate sponsors, who decide to support this team and any other campaigns that commit to having women on their rosters. And, it's up to those other campaigns to give women a fair shot. Most importantly, the future depends on women being willing to believe in themselves, trust one another, and extend their reach.